How Different It Was

How Different It Was

CANADIANS AT THE TIME
OF CONFEDERATION

MICHAEL J. GOODSPEED

DUNDURN
A J. PATRICK BOYER BOOK
TORONTO

Cover image: Library and Archive Canada Storing block ice at Nun's Island, Montréal, by Duncan, James D.
Printer: Webcom

Library and Archives Canada Cataloguing in Publication

Goodspeed, Michael J. (Michael James), 1951-, author
    How different it was : Canadians at the time of confederation / Michael J. Goodspeed.

Includes bibliographical references and index.
Issued in print and electronic formats.
ISBN 978-1-4597-3694-8 (softcover).--ISBN 978-1-4597-3695-5 (PDF).--
ISBN 978-1-4597-3696-2 (EPUB)

    1. Canada--History--1867-. 2. Canada--Social life and customs.
3. National characteristics, Canadian--History. I. Title.

FC500.G66 2017   971.05   C2017-900759-9
                                              C2017-900760-2

1 2 3 4 5   21 20 19 18 17

Conseil des Arts du Canada   Canada Council for the Arts   Canada   ONTARIO ARTS COUNCIL CONSEIL DES ARTS DE L'ONTARIO an Ontario government agency un organisme du gouvernement de l'Ontario

We acknowledge the support of the **Canada Council for the Arts** and the **Ontario Arts Council** for our publishing program. We also acknowledge the financial support of the **Government of Ontario**, through the **Ontario Book Publishing Tax Credit** and the **Ontario Media Development Corporation**, and the **Government of Canada**.

VISIT US AT

dundurn.com | @dundurnpress | dundurnpress | dundurnpress

Dundurn
3 Church Street, Suite 500
Toronto, Ontario, Canada
M5E 1M2

For my grandsons, Euan Tomos Goodspeed and Jovan James Lazic:
may their Canada be tolerant, free, just, and prosperous.

Table of Contents

Introduction

Walter Ferguson was a farmer. He was in many ways like most other British North Americans in 1864. He had sixty acres of fields and a wood lot on the Rustico Road north of Charlottetown, Prince Edward Island. Like most of his neighbours in the last days of that sweltering summer, he had no intention of missing the biggest show in decades. The Olympic Circus from Philadelphia was in town. The show was advertised as having acrobats, trick riders, clowns, dancing dogs, and performing monkeys. Walter had never seen anything like it, and he was thrilled that his family would have the chance to see such an extraordinary performance. The only other circus to come to Prince Edward Island had visited over twenty years before, and in those days his family couldn't afford to take the time off or pay the price of a ticket.[1]

Like most Islanders, seeing the circus meant a small financial sacrifice on Walter's part. The Fergusons weren't poor, yet Walter knew that if he took the whole family, he'd have to find the money somewhere — which was fine. His old coat could probably last another winter.

At nine that September morning there wasn't a cloud in the sky. It had been a hot summer, and today was going to be another scorcher. Walter straightened his draft mare's handmade harness and bellyband and cinched her securely to the farm wagon. If it got too hot he'd have to stop and water the horse half way to town. Even with the water stop, they would get to town with a little time to spare. With everything ready, Walter helped his wife and the remaining five children up onto the open wagon.

The Fergusons were frugal people. Early this morning, Walter's wife, Ruth, had packed their lunch in a wicker basket. The road to Charlottetown was heavily wash-boarded at this time of the year — but with luck, the wagon shaking from the dirt road wouldn't break the wax seal on the two jars of glass-stoppered pickles. It would be a shame to have their sandwiches ruined.

The damp tea towels that had been wrapped around the pickle jars would help a little to protect them. The cold tea made the night before was safely corked inside thick glass bottles. It was going to be a wonderful day.

The Olympic Circus took place in Charlottetown at the same time as the conference for the union of Britain's North American colonies. Like most Canadians, Walter had only a passing interest in grandiose politics of the kind that involved the politicians in Charlottetown. As things turned out, the conference passed without much to-do. The politicians worked out the conditions for what would eventually become a united Canada, and Walter's family loved the circus.

Walter would not find himself a Canadian citizen until 1873, when P.E.I. finally joined Canada. By then, the country stretched from the Atlantic Ocean to the Pacific and, while he had a great deal in common with his compatriots in the other provinces, the regional circumstances of each of the future provinces differed in many ways. And although conditions varied in each region, each colony shared a common economic rationale for joining a Canadian union: by themselves, the regions were just too small to exist independently. They needed one another, and their differences were not nearly as large as the ones that existed between themselves and the Americans or British.

Canadians differed from Britain and America in many ways. Canadian society varied in terms of class, its economic basis, regionalism, cultural outlook, its security issues, and its levels of urbanization and industrialization.

Canadians treated minorities differently than the British and Americans. Canadian attitudes to the arts, public institutions, education, the role of tradition, and the nature of civil society were all substantially different than those of the British and Americans.

During the Confederation decades, Britain's North American colonies were outwardly quiet, seemingly stable, and relatively peaceful. Although the American economy was booming, America was reeling from the human and material costs of a devastating civil war, as well as struggling with massive economic reconstruction. The United States had already eclipsed Britain in terms of population and manufacturing output, while the British "mother country," on the other hand, was, throughout the Confederation era, newly industrialized and caught up in the fervour of the fastest and largest imperial expansion in history. Amongst all three countries there were shared similarities, but there were also massively dissimilar features and circumstances at play.

Perhaps the most important differences were that Britain's North American colonies had a small population and were geographically isolated. America, in contrast, with a surging population, was ten times larger than the colonies. As a result, in British and American eyes, Canada was relatively insignificant. It was a small, peaceful, colonial dependency, perched on the edge of the wilderness. Yet, as result of this very detachment, the colonies were growing, forging their own character with unique ideas, customs, institutions, fears, and aspirations.

There were common features shared amongst Britain's North American colonies, but each had its own unique character; and at the outset of the Confederation decades, the very thought of joining them together to form one truly independent country straddled the borderline of being disloyal. Few Canadian citizens actually considered Canada as a full-fledged country. As late as 1891, in a burst of imperial zeal, John A. Macdonald proclaimed, "A British subject I was born, a British subject I will die." Decades before, in making the case for Confederation, he was unequivocal as to how he envisaged Canadians being "a subordinate, but still powerful people."[2]

Most Canadians, before and after Confederation, regarded the country as "a self-governing British colony"[3] — about as incongruous a description of independence as one can imagine. Canada certainly had some degree of independence, but as a country it was willingly subordinate to its wealthier and more powerful parent, letting Britain take charge in matters of defence and foreign policy, and have the ultimate authority over its laws. From today's perspective, such an abdication of responsibility might seem a bit absurd and a touch juvenile, but given that Canada had no external enemies, was geographically isolated, and had a trusting nature, that kind of cheerful national adolescence was understandable.

Getting the mail from mainland Canada to P.E.I. was often a struggle, as this illustration of Royal Mail delivery in the winter of 1867 shows.

The colonies that were to make up modern Canada were as peaceful as anywhere on earth. This is not to say the region was without problems. It was just that the inhabitants of Upper and Lower Canada and the Maritimes were much like Walter Ferguson. They led peaceful, relatively prosperous lives, and for the most part were optimistic about their future. The Canadian colonies had no serious external threats and were sheltered by what its residents saw as a benevolent and protective motherland.

As Canadians, we have often prided ourselves on this peaceful legacy, yet we should be careful not to be smug. Canada's relative tolerance and prosperity has been more a product of chance than of any shrewd decisions our ancestors made.

Along with a small handful of other nations, Canada has been the beneficiary of tremendous good luck. Free from external threats and relatively self-sufficient, Canada has, for the most part, been an enormously privileged society. And despite several shortcomings, it has, through good fortune, progressed steadily toward realizing its potential. The creation of prosperous societies marked by compassion, fairness, and equality has been a slow and difficult journey for most of mankind. In this respect, Canada in the Confederation decades enjoyed several advantages over much of the rest of the world.

Chapter One

BACKGROUND TO A NEW NATION

Between 1840 and 1880, Canadians were fortunate enough to live relatively unhindered by much of the turmoil that characterized the rest of the world. Canada had no external security vulnerabilities. The country had few conflicting venomous ideologies, or religious or ethnic tensions that threatened to tear it apart. There were no debilitating class conflicts, and such regional rivalries as existed were mild and certainly not violent. However, as we will see in later chapters, Canada had its share of bigotry, intolerance, and foolishness.

By 1840, Canada was well on its way to establishing the cultural and political foundations of a modern nation. But before examining particular aspects of mid-nineteenth-century Canadian society in detail, and at the risk of oversimplifying history, we should briefly examine the situation in which Canadians found themselves in the years leading to Confederation.

The circumstances of First Nations and other aboriginal peoples will be examined later with each of the country's regions, but in broad terms, aboriginal Canadians, Canada's first inhabitants, were largely ignored in the years prior to Confederation. That wasn't always the case. Up until the War of 1812, in the web of alliances negotiated between the French, the British, and the Americans, First Nations were militarily useful to the various colonists and, as a result, were treated as a more influential partner. But with political stability and the increasing industrialization that followed the war, the status of aboriginal peoples began to decline. By the outset of the Confederation decades, First Nations peoples found themselves completely marginalized.

This change in status marked a sudden shift from the status quo that existed in North America before the arrival of European colonists. Aboriginal Canadians are believed to have arrived from Asia ten thousand years

Nineteenth-century Inuit seal hunting party.

ago. Anthropologists believe that the ancestors of the aboriginal population of North America migrated across the Bering Strait that separates Siberia from Alaska during the last ice age and established societies in the traditional regions that Europeans found them in prior to and after the fifteenth century.

Canada's first peoples have been classified according to geography, into seven very broad major groupings.*

---

* Among Canada's aboriginal communities there are over 600 identifiable tribal, linguistic, and cultural groupings. Reducing these to seven major categories is a necessary but regrettable distortion.

The Inuit were in the Arctic region and right across the Canadian North. In the Sub-Arctic were First Nations such as the Innu and the Dene, the Cree, the Ojibwa, the Atikamekw, and the Beothuk. Out on the Pacific Coast were a highly differentiated mix of linguistic and cultural bands that lived in what is now coastal British Columbia. In the high plateau areas and adjoining regions of the interior of British Columbia lived the Southern Dene and the numerous branches of the Athabaskan peoples. On the Prairies lived diverse bands of Plains First Nations, which included groups such as the Blackfoot, the Plains Cree, the Ojibwa, and the Assiniboine peoples. Further east, in a region thousands of kilometres wide and consisting of numerous tribal and linguistic groups, were the highly varied First Nations of the Eastern Woodlands. This last group consisted of a very broad range of peoples and cultures that included many different tribes of the Algonquian peoples, the Huron, the Iroquois, the Woodland Cree, and Ojibwa tribes, as well as the Maliseet and Mi'kmaq nations. The Métis, a mixed society that grew from the merging of First Nations peoples and European fur traders, lived primarily on the Prairies, and had rapidly established themselves as a unique and distinct culture in the late eighteenth century.

Although population estimates vary, it is widely accepted that at the time of the first European settlements there were approximately half a million aboriginals living in several hundred tribal groupings in what is now Canada. Aboriginal populations were subject to their own dynamic changes and there were several major ongoing migrations amongst indigenous peoples prior to and just after the arrival of Europeans, but these changes were minor in comparison with what was to follow: the lifestyles, the locations, the health and security, and the cultures of all the aboriginal peoples were to change even more drastically over the next three hundred years.

The second group of founding peoples, the French, began to arrive in the early seventeenth century. French migration started with an annual journey of fishing boats to the Grand Banks off the coast of Newfoundland. Shortly thereafter, the lure of the fur trade and the beginnings of European imperial expansion soon saw thriving settlements established at Quebec, along the St. Lawrence, and in the Maritimes.

During the period of French colonization in Canada, the British established colonies south of the area controlled by the French, in what is the present-day eastern United States. The settlement of this area by the British was not accomplished without significant resistance from the resident aboriginal populations, and the period was characterized by a ragged and seemingly interminable succession of wars between the British and First Nations.

French expansion in North America stopped abruptly with the British seizure of Quebec in 1759 and the subsequent Treaty of Paris in 1763. With the Treaty of Paris, most merchants, civil administrators, and the military garrison chose to return to France, leaving behind *habitant** farmers and their Catholic clergy.

It was a migration that was to have a defining effect on the nature of French-Canadian society for almost two hundred years. From 1763 until well into the very late nineteenth century, the French-speaking peoples of Canada led a generally quiet life under British rule. Allowed to keep their language, laws and religion, the remaining 70,000 French inhabitants of Quebec and the Maritimes lived a peaceful existence in a unique and predominantly rural culture.

---

* The term *habitant* was of seventeenth-century origin and referred to the class of francophone Quebecers who made their living doing agricultural work in seigneuries. Over the years, it has evolved into an affectionate term for rural French-speaking Quebecers and is symbolic of the hardy and spirited lifestyle of early Quebec.

English-speaking Canadians had somewhat more diverse origins. One of the first handful of such immigrants to the Canadas were discharged British soldiers — mostly from the Fraser Highlanders, one of the units that participated in the Battle for Quebec. These men stayed on as a part of the first British garrison, and after their regiment was disbanded, many of its soldiers moved to the area near Rivière-du-Loup. They married local women and were almost all assimilated into the larger French culture. It wasn't until the American Revolution that large numbers of English-speaking immigrants began to settle in Canada. In a series of waves, 100,000 United Empire Loyalists emigrated to Canada. Loyal to the British Crown, they settled in the Maritimes, in Quebec's Eastern Townships, and on the northern shore of Lake Ontario. Amongst the many legacies left by these people, one of the most evident and enduring ones was that, ever since, Canadian English has had a North American accent rather than a British one.

With the British division of Quebec in 1791 into Upper and Lower Canada, English-speaking immigrants were allowed to live under British institutions and laws in Upper Canada, while Lower Canadians could maintain their French civil code with protections given in law to their Catholic religion. At a time characterized by intense and often violent religious intolerance, it was a remarkably broad-minded proposal, but as a solution to the colonial management of these two regions, it soon proved to be inadequate.

Shortly after the establishment of Upper Canada, which roughly covered what is now southern Ontario, there was an immediate increase in British immigration.

At the same time, the population of Upper Canada and Lower Canada's Eastern Townships continued to swell with a continuous stream of land-hungry settlers from the United States. At the same time as this massive English-speaking migration was taking place, the French-speaking population of Lower Canada grew steadily as a result of high birth rates and falling mortality rates. Canada's total population by 1840 had grown to just under 1.2 million people.

Despite the economic growth that accompanied this rapid increase in population, critical political grievances festered. Colonial governance in Upper and Lower Canada was not harsh, but it was burdensome, discriminatory, and irritatingly autocratic. The appointed executive branches of government in both provinces operated as self-serving oligarchies that frequently chose to ignore their elected legislative assemblies. Insurrections demanding reform in the two provinces in 1837 and 1838 were almost inevitable.

These rebellions were indifferently supported by much of the population, and the rebels in both provinces were badly organized and poorly led. The government handily defeated the rebels. By comparison with contemporary uprisings elsewhere, particularly in Europe, Canada's troubles were relatively minor. But these insurrections were not entirely bloodless. In Lower Canada, over three hundred men died in various skirmishes, and in total more than one hundred leaders were subsequently transported to Australia. A handful were executed. It was a tense and unstable time that could have spiraled into much broader and more violent civil war.

Robert-Shore-Milnes Bouchette, one of Lower Canada's Patriote rebels, in prison in 1838. Bouchette was eventually exiled to Bermuda. He returned to Canada in 1845 and went on to have a distinguished career in the Canadian civil service.

Not wanting to repeat the mistakes of the American Revolution, the British sent Lord Durham out to assess the situation. He travelled to the two colonies, listened to the locals, and drafted his conclusions for bringing peace and prosperity to the region. His famous report became the basis for the "Act of Union," which established a kind of lopsided, semi-responsible government in a newly united Canada. In addition to governing these two colonies as a single entity, Durham's plan was also designed to assimilate the French Canadians. Lower Canada became Canada East, and, although it had a substantially larger population, it was given the same number of seats in the legislature as Upper Canada, which became Canada West.

It is worthwhile putting the geographic context of the Act of Union into perspective. If you look at a modern map of Canada, Durham's newly united Canada only occupied a tiny fraction of Canada's current land mass. It consisted of what is now southern Ontario and southern Quebec. The remainder of Britain's North American colonies were all distinct and separate entities. These other British possessions consisted of "Rupert's Land," which was a massive tract consisting of all the lands that drained into Hudson's Bay, all of which were administered by the Hudson's Bay Company. To the west was the largely unexplored "New Caledonia," which equated roughly to what is now British Columbia and northern Oregon. To the east were the separate British colonies of Newfoundland, New Brunswick, Prince Edward Island, and Nova Scotia.

In demographic terms, the Act of Union was clearly unfair. It was designed with the impractical and potentially explosive aim of assimilating the larger and culturally vigorous French-Canadian population. Surprisingly though, for a period, the new "self-governing colony" functioned reasonably well.

This skewed governmental arrangement worked because, despite what other prejudices and shortcomings the legislators of the time might have had, the elected leaders of the two colonies understood that the two communities were bound together as if in a three-legged race. In both Canada East and Canada West there were sensible political leaders who appreciated that the path to peace, prosperity, and growth lay in co-operation with one another.

There was also another element at play. The key legislators had a practical sense of fairness. As a matter of common sense, the majority of Canadians in both camps realized that the more populated Canada East was unlikely to be assimilated by Canada West, and that given the violence of the recent past, it would ultimately be foolhardy to attempt such an undertaking.

There were other indications of a shared and progressive public spirit. Although it was bitterly resented by many, the rebels from the uprisings of 1837 and 1838 were eventually pardoned and reparations were made for losses incurred in the fighting. This decision was the result of a sensible desire to get the violence behind them, but it was also a clear indication that the temper of the times was changing. The period's demands for increased political rights, public education, electoral changes, the beginnings of social welfare, and increased agitation for the abolition of the slave trade had their own distinct echoes in the Canadian context. Lastly, and perhaps most importantly, French-Canadian politicians wisely saw this arrangement as a temporary one, and were shrewd and patient enough to work peacefully for an equitable solution that would provide them the best chance for their culture's survival.

Despite all this, it would be wrong to assume that Confederation in 1867 was driven exclusively by influences that were uniquely Canadian. There were several critical, externally imposed issues that pushed Canada to the larger federated union. Not the least of these was that Britain, which was also changing, was changing its attitudes to its colonies.

As loyal as Anglo-Canadians were to the mother country, that affection was not always reciprocated in the same measure. British economic thinking was evolving, and in its northern cities a school of economic thought called "Manchesterism" emerged. Free trade was one of the key elements of this doctrine; and amongst other tenets was the belief that artificial trade barriers, such as duties, were impediments to wealth creation, and so restrictive trade laws had to be liberalized. Amongst other things, those advocating for Manchesterism called for the repeal of the preferential rates given to wheat grown in the colonies. Up until this time, Canadian farmers had reaped a handsome profit by offsetting the costs of trans-Atlantic shipping and selling their wheat tariff-free in Britain. That profitable relationship ended abruptly in 1846 when the British government repealed the "Corn Laws." At the same time, due to poor crop yields in Ontario, Quebec, and the United States, the Canadian economy went into a recession. Popular Canadian opinion blamed the economic troubles squarely on the repeal of the Corn Laws.

If the repeal of the Corn Laws resulted in economic difficulty for those in British North America, the considerable benefits of industrialization also began to transform Canadian society. Mass-produced consumer goods, along with steam ships and railways, stimulated trade and vastly improved standards of living.

One of the immediate consequences of these changes was that politicians and businessmen realized they needed larger domestic markets to ensure prosperity. Many believed that continued growth and economic security could only be brought about through the political union of all of Britain's North American colonies.

Any such political union, however, made absolutely no sense within the existing structure of a unified Canada East and Canada West. Political union, if it was to have sufficient mass to be effective, had to include Britain's North Atlantic colonies of New Brunswick, Nova Scotia and P.E.I. And because the St. Lawrence River froze in the winter, effectively bringing trade to a halt for several months each year, commercial ties between Canada and the Maritimes only made sense if there were railway linkages, and in the case of Newfoundland, improved oceangoing communications. It was all a wonderful prescription for internally generated economic growth, and a tremendous opportunity to fix the lopsided and highly centrist form of governance that Lord Durham had devised during his brief tenure in the colony.

Another unanticipated consequence of Britain repealing the Corn Laws was that it eroded the loyalty and commitment that preferential market access had promoted. By distancing itself economically from its colonies, Britain now exercised considerably less influence in its overseas possessions. In Canada, smarting from a trade rebuff, there was a new spirit of determination and self-confidence. With the collapse of overseas markets, colonial leaders became more self-reliant by necessity. It was a heady feeling, and many Canadian politicians savoured this new-found sensation of independence.

Although in English Canada popular sentiment at the time was brashly imperial and patriotic, astute Canadian business and political leaders were in no doubt about the true nature of the British Empire. In economic and emotional terms, India was unquestionably the coveted jewel in the British Empire's crown. By comparison, all Britain's North American colonies were only slightly larger in population than the city of London. And in terms of trade, the southern United States was viewed as a much more important and indispensable link to the booming textile industries that lay at the heart of Britain's economy.

Like neglected suitors, it began to gradually dawn on the established colonies that in the mid-nineteenth century, Canada, Australia, and New Zealand were more valuable to Britain as convenient destinations to ship large numbers of its restive and unemployable populations. It was an arrangement that served Canada's purposes brilliantly, but it wasn't flattering. The "self-governing colonies" were a ready-made pressure release for starving Irish families, for Scotland's evicted tenants, and those with limited prospects in England's teeming industrial cities. And like a wistful suitor, Canadians gradually came to the conclusion that life could be better with a new and more stable arrangement that more suited her needs.

The evolving colonial relationship with Britain was important, but it wasn't the only factor prompting change. The American Civil War had a profound effect on Canada. By 1861, America was larger and more powerful than Britain. And by the war's end in 1865, no one could possibly dispute that a truly awe-inspiring

Confederation-era Canadians took their politics seriously. A typical election speech, in 1860s Quebec.

military and industrial power had emerged on Canada's southern border. America possessed the most modern, well-trained, well-equipped, and battle hardened army in the world. During the Civil War, Britain had antagonized the North, and America was in an expansionist mood. It was an uncomfortable time to be a British colony next to the U.S.A.

Even when that military threat abated, the United States was still seen as dangerous by many Canadians because of the potential influence it possessed as a result of its economic might and cultural prominence. Still, Canada's relationship with the United States was much more complex than superficial appearances would indicate. Despite America's proximity, size, and the large numbers of American immigrants in Canada,

U.S. influence in the Confederation decades was substantially less than it is today. Canada was still largely British in outlook and had not developed any true sense of Canadian identity, which is not to say Canadians were not concerned by American influence. For example, in 1850 authorities in Upper Canada were worried that 40 percent of the school texts used in Canada West were American in origin. There were a host of similar issues looming on the horizon.

It was clear that by mid-century, America was emerging as one of the most dynamic societies on the globe. During Canada's Confederation decades, the United States was in the throes of three wrenching, nation-altering events: America was dealing with the effects of the abolition of slavery and the Civil War; the country was in the midst of an unprecedented industrial and population boom; and throughout the period, the United States was aggressively expanding her territory. Each of these issues had profound effects on Canada.

For Canada, the Civil War was the most important of these events. While most Canadians were overwhelmingly opposed to slavery, the country was not unanimously pro-Northern in its outlook. As a British colony, Canada was officially neutral, but the views of many Canadians reflected attitudes in the mother country. The British textile industry was dependent on Southern cotton, which greatly influenced British leanings and led to several diplomatic and non-violent naval confrontations. In Quebec many identified with the South as an underdog that was ruled by a larger and more powerful majority. In the other English-speaking colonies, more than a few were hostile to the North as a result of truculent annexationists

like William Seward, who openly promoted the forcible seizure of Canada. In Saint John, New Brunswick, a city that boasted of being the home and temporary wartime refuge of wealthy Southern families, parades were held to celebrate Confederate military victories. In several other locations, active pro-Confederate organizations operated freely out of Canada. The Copperhead Movement, which consisted of prominent Northerners who advocated Southern succession and an immediate end to the war, overtly ran their headquarters from Windsor, Ontario. In Toronto, it was an open secret that Southern subversives plotting acts of sabotage across the North operated out of the city's hotels. And, most famously, in 1864 Confederate soldiers launched the St. Alban's Raid, robbing Vermont banks and then retreating back into Quebec where they were arrested, and to the outrage of the North, freed on a legal technicality.

On the other hand, the vast majority of Canadians found slavery completely repugnant and supported the Union efforts. Canadian attitudes to American slavery had deep roots. Assisted by Northern abolitionists, upward of sixty thousand fugitive black slaves found a safe haven in Canada via the Underground Railroad. Support for the abolition of slavery also had a practical and unofficial military dimension. More than forty thousand English- and French-speaking Canadians served voluntarily in the Union Army. This was a truly astounding number for such a small country, especially one that was neutral. At the war's outset it equated to just over 5 percent of the available fighting-age male population.

Nonetheless, when the American Civil War ended, Canadians were justifiably anxious about the military threat posed by a powerful, million-man army to the south of them. Lurking beneath America's new military might was the recurrent but hazy threat of continentalism. For some Americans, the occupation of the entire North American continent was viewed as a sanctified obligation; for many of them, it was a dream that had never really died. John L. O'Sullivan, an influential journalist and typically ardent advocate of continentalism, had once proclaimed America's "manifest destiny to overspread and to possess the whole of the continent which Providence has given us for the development of the great experiment of liberty and federated self-government entrusted to us."[1]

This hallowed and mystical belief in continental domination was profoundly disturbing for Canadians. Many remembered the Mexican-American War that had taken place only eighteen years previously. Since that time, Texas, California, Nevada, New Mexico, Arizona, Utah, Washington, and Oregon had been annexed by the United States. In the years following the Civil War, there were influential voices in the northern states who were openly advocating occupying Canada.

The threat of annexation by the United States was a persistent theme in American political discourse. As early as 1818, the Anglo-American Convention established the border between the United States and British North America. It was agreed that the border would run from the 49th parallel between Lake of the Woods and the Pacific Ocean with a temporary joint claim established over the Oregon territory. However, in 1844, James Polk ran his election campaign with the belligerent slogan of "54° 40' or Fight." It never came to

war, and in 1846 the boundary was once again settled at the 49th parallel. Nonetheless the renewed threat of the seizure of Britain's "empty" territory beyond Canada West remained a further stimulus for Confederation.

Throughout the war, William Seward, the North's fiery secretary of state, often spoke rapturously of American territory running from Manitoba to British Columbia and up into Alaska. In Canada, Seward's outbursts triggered alarm, but perhaps even more disturbing to Canadians were the periodic editorials that cropped up in major British newspapers that proposed Britain placate the Americans by acquiescing to Seward's schemes.

One of the reasons that the notion of continental domination had never died was that for many Americans, despite international treaties, the border with Canada was not viewed as the same kind of institutional barrier as it is today. This was largely a result of the porous nature of the border. Throughout the Confederation decades, the border posed no real impediment to movement, and Americans and Canadians migrated back and forth across it freely. Americans for the most part sought free farmland, while Canadians were lured south in large numbers by the possibility of employment in the rapidly industrializing northern states. Records itemizing the precise numbers of Canadian migrants to America are unreliable, but the numbers involved were substantial.

However much Canadians feared annexation by the United States, to the point that it became a key factor driving Confederation, in truth, in the post-Civil War United States, it never reached a serious planning phase. And fortunately, President Andrew Johnson, the man who succeeded Lincoln, had no intention of going to war with Britain. Like Johnson, most Americans focused their attentions on the issues of post-war reconstruction and westward expansion.

Yet while the conventional military threat from America's army subsided, the Fenian Brotherhood, a paramilitary organization made up of Irish veterans from the Union Army, posed a more realistic problem. The Fenians, with several thousand volunteers, hoped to seize Canada and barter the country for Irish independence. The Fenians were never strong enough to occupy Canada, but they posed a menace to peace and threatened to destabilize international relations. In total, the Fenians made five largely chaotic and unsuccessful incursions into Canada. Thirty-two Canadian militiamen died repelling them. Although the raids never materialized as a major military threat, they proved to be a powerful stimulus for Confederation, for they underscored the need for a co-ordinated colonial defence plan.

The end of the Civil War also had major implications for British North America in terms of trade. Trade with the United States has always been a critical issue for Canadians, and fluctuating American demand for Canadian products accentuated the boom and bust nature of Canada's economic circumstances. For many Canadians, the Civil War represented a time of economic opportunity. Canada prospered during the Civil War, selling ships, agricultural produce, and manufactured goods primarily to the North. For many Canadians, the Civil War meant newly invigorated markets for shipments of everything from grain, timber, leather products, cavalry horses, coal, and iron ore. It

M. Chamberlain, a Canadian militia soldier from the 60th Battalion, who fought in the Fenian Raids.

was a boom time that wasn't bound to last. Resentful of Britain and fuelled by nationalist feeling, a year after the Civil War ended the Americans cancelled the free trade arrangements that had existed since the Reciprocity Treaty of 1854. It was a devastating blow, and Canadians were forced to find internal markets for their goods.

Politically, the war also exerted a strong influence on Britain's North American colonies. From a constitutional perspective, the divisive issue of American states' rights overshadowed the tone of Confederation. And the Fathers of Confederation, anxious to avoid the American example and the possibility of civil war, were in agreement that the new country should be a carefully defined federation that was to be built upon the principles of peace, order, and good government.

While America was certainly the strongest external influence in the development of the Canadian state, to get a sense of who Canadians were in the Confederation decades, it is equally important to understand Canada's situation in relation to its place in the larger global setting.

Chapter Two

THE VICTORIAN OUTLOOK

Perhaps the two most prominent concepts that infused the character of the period were Christianity and a new-found acceptance of science.

In the mid-nineteenth century, Christian sensibilities pervaded and influenced virtually every aspect of social, economic, and political life. Christian faith permeated almost all aspects of Canadian life. It was a time when the vast majority of citizens attended church every Sunday and sermons were regularly and fervently discussed, reprinted, and often widely distributed. Compared to modern Canada, with its more accommodating attitudes of tolerance, understanding, and secular civic values, the Christian certainty and uncompromising world view of the Confederation decades stands in vivid contrast.

The period of the Confederation decades was above all a Christian era, but it was simultaneously a time of tremendous scientific change as well as a period of discovery. For example, Louis Pasteur discovered the principles of vaccination, microbial fermentation, and pasteurization. Charles Darwin published his revolutionary theory of evolution, *On the Origin of Species*, and the era was characterized by a flurry of inventions that took the world in radically new directions: the telegraph, the sewing machine, the internal combustion engine, the Gatling gun, railways, steam ships, gas lighting, and the telephone were all inventions that came of age alongside the period when Canada became a nation.

The word "scientist" first came into common usage during the Confederation decades. It was an era where scientific and technological change intersected with social change. The study of "natural philosophy" and "natural history," fields of learning that still had a vaguely medieval ring to them, were distilled into "science." It was a period that marked the passage of science moving from being a part-time diversion for eccentric gentlemen to a legitimate profession for scientists.

Despite the new emphasis on scientific method and evidence-based reasoning, science and traditional religious faith managed to co-exist throughout the Victorian age. New certainties grew out of this union of scientific reasoning and traditional faith. Western belief in Christianity as the only "true" religion and an unchallenged conviction in the supremacy of European races and culture, coupled with the power of Western military and industrial inventions, allowed the fiercely nationalistic and imperialist features of Western societies to evolve and flourish.

In spite of this new-found confidence Victorians were still very much aware of what they didn't know. Much of the world still remained a mystery to Europeans and most nations were keen to plant their flag on these "undiscovered lands." Vast tracts of the globe and most of the interior of Canada had not been mapped.

It was no coincidence that the explorer David Livingstone was lionized in the press; and to many Canadians, as well as to the rest of the world, he personified the period's ideal character. From the age of ten, Livingstone worked twelve hours a day in a cotton mill, yet he still managed to study for a university degree. Tremendous personal energy and an unquenchable thirst for knowledge combined with profound religious zeal led him to become a missionary and an explorer. He disappeared for six years covering vast tracks of previously unchartered Africa. He died pursuing his twin dreams of discovery and Christian evangelization. Perhaps more than any other man of the time, Livingstone exemplified the age's merging of empire, faith, and scientific exploration. Not surprisingly, in keeping with the spirit of the age, his personal motto was "Christianity, Commerce, and Civilization."

The roots of Canada's current population extend deep into every corner of the world. To better appreciate Canada's situation during this period, we should understand how the new nation related to the rest of the world.

Throughout the Confederation decades, despite the growing influence of the United States, the country that wielded the most social influence on Canada was Britain. Like so much of the world during this time, Britain was undergoing tremendous internal change.

The effects of religion and science certainly had a powerful influence in shaping the character of the time, but in Britain the political notions of utilitarianism also had a profound effect on the nature and direction of government, and on all aspects of life. Utilitarianism is the ethical theory, largely put forth by Jeremy Bentham and John Stuart Mill, that man's actions should be devoted to obtaining the greatest utility, or "happiness," for the greatest number of people. As an underlying philosophy, utilitarianism has been credited with developing modern ideas of social conscience and social justice, and, less favourably, with advancing an "end justifies the means" world view, one which sanctioned the most ruthless aspects of industrialization and the spread of imperialism.

Whatever the role of utilitarianism, the two most prominent aspects of British national life in this period were the industrialization of society and the growth of empire. Technological developments in what has been called the "Second Industrial Revolution" saw the increased use of new technologies: railways, telegraph, steam-driven manufacturing, the development of machine tools, the mass production of steel, and urban developments, such as the wide-spread introduction of gas, water, and sewage systems.* With these developments Britain became one of the world's most powerful nations. Her economic strength enabled her to expand her overseas influence.

With a relatively small professional army and the world's most powerful navy, Britain managed to subdue and control huge swaths of the globe. The nineteenth century, for good reason, has been dubbed Britain's "Imperial Century." Up to a quarter of the globe's land surface and a fifth of the world's population were subject to British rule. Most Britons regarded it as a golden age. For many at home in Britain, the mid-Victorian period was regarded as an era of peace. In fact, Britain was involved almost constantly in a series of small, regional, colonial campaigns and interventions in far-flung places such as Afghanistan, Australia, Bhutan, Burma, Canada, China, Crimea, Ghana, India, Japan, Malaysia, New Zealand, South Africa, and Sudan.

All these military interventions were viewed as being entirely legitimate. At the time, not just the British but virtually all Western nations readily accepted racist interpretations of Darwin's theory of evolution as

a justification for imperialism. Few Britons, or for that matter the inhabitants of her white colonies, disputed this world view. Goldwin Smith, a popular historian of the time and a self-proclaimed anti-imperialist, trumpeted about the imperial spirit, "It is the noblest the world has seen.... Never had there been such an attempt to make conquest the servant of civilization. About keeping India there is no question. England has a real duty there."[1]

In a ruthlessly practical sense, the notion of empire was simply accepted as a lucrative and natural economic system wherein colonies existed to provide raw materials and ready-made markets for the industrialized mother country. Rudyard Kipling, British imperialism's most ardent literary proponent, captured the spirit of imperial dominance in his poem "Screw-Guns." The poem was turned into a popular song and sung cheerfully across the British Empire in music halls, schools, homes, and pubs. Its chorus cheerfully urging native tribesmen to:

Jest send in your Chief an' surrender — it's
worse if you fights or you runs:
    You can go where you please, you can
skid up the trees, but you don't get away
from the guns!

Yet another element of imperialism that strikes twenty-first-century sensibilities as outrageous: possessing colonies was seen as a national duty. Again, Rudyard Kipling curtly summed up this assumed obligation, calling it "the white man's burden." Imperial domination

---

* The First Industrial Revolution was characterized by the increased use of coal, iron, and steel in the manufacture of new machinery such as looms and agricultural tools. The Second Industrial Revolution, which roughly corresponds with the first three decades of the Confederation era, saw the introduction of steam-driven machinery and transport.

These four men were riverboat steamer captains and volunteered in the Nile Expedition to relieve General Gordon in 1884. In a burst of imperial enthusiasm, 386 civilian Canadians volunteered to assist the British Army in getting down the Nile. The Canadians were known as the "Nile Voyageurs."

some colonies got the benefit of an efficient civil service, a well-established legal system, roads, railways, and education systems, these came at an appalling cost.

The period outlook considered violent domination of weaker societies as entirely normal. It was a perspective that was profoundly different from what we would like to think are twenty-first-century Western ideas of justice, equality, independence, and international law. And, while the concept of forcibly creating an empire is generally abhorrent to modern sensibilities, for nineteenth-century Europeans it was neither shameful nor novel. All major European powers had rapacious empires. It was what technologically advanced societies of the time did. And despite its smug sense of pre-eminence, viewed in its wider historical context, the British Empire was less oppressive than those of other European nations; and it was nowhere near as homicidal or as cruel as previous empires. The British Empire was saintly in comparison to the Persians, the Romans, the Byzantines, the Mongols, or the Umayyad or Ottoman Caliphates that preceded it — or even the Soviet Empire that followed it.

It wasn't just the pride in empire that helped shape the Canadian character. Demographic changes in Britain in the mid-nineteenth century exerted a profound effect on her colonies. Even despite massive emigration to the New World, the population of Britain in the Confederation decades soared from eighteen million to almost thirty million people. Rapid industrialization changed the face of Britain's cities. In the rural areas, disruptive changes to farming technologies in the form of mechanization and improved fertilizers

was viewed by most people of the time as an onerously provided benefit conferred by "superior" races upon "primitive" nations in order to spread the advantages of "civilization" and good government. While it is true forced much of the population to leave their traditional lifestyles on farms and country villages for low-paying wages in crowded cities.

Despite the massive growth and subsequent dislocation in its population during this period, Britain was notable amongst European nations for keeping its rigid pre-industrial-era class system largely intact. British society was remarkably stable and relatively insulated from the violent upheavals and revolutionary change experienced by most other European powers. This was a result of two factors. Emigration provided a ready outlet for restive and economically trapped populations, and attitudes in Britain's system of parliamentary government evolved, allowing for political, economic, social, and labour reforms. This culture and its traditions were reflected, and to some extent magnified, in the more socially tranquil Canadian context.

Despite reform, mid-nineteenth-century Britain had many serious issues. Urban poverty was rampant, hunger and malnutrition were widespread, housing for much of the population was abysmal, public health was a major problem, child mortality levels were high, and many of those fortunate enough to have steady jobs worked mercilessly long hours in grinding and often dangerous conditions.

There were also enormous contradictions in British society at the time. Strong moral and religious undercurrents advocated progressive change; but these attitudes existed alongside traditional attitudes of indifference to the poor. Socially conservative thought held that responsibilities to the poor and disadvantaged were not something governments became involved in, but were things that should lie entirely with individuals or with charitable private institutions. This began to change as increased literacy in Victorian Britain led to greater social activism. By the outset of the Confederation decades, poor laws had been enacted, Catholics had been granted full legal rights, child labour had been partially restricted, and electoral reforms had increased the numbers and classes of people who could vote.

Most of these views were enthusiastically reflected in Canadian society. However, they existed alongside other, more crippling attitudes. For most Canadians, social responsibility did not extend beyond one's class or region; work was considered a sacred duty that was good for the soul; and poverty was widely viewed as an individual choice based on lack of thrift, indolence, irresponsible habits, and low character.

Chapter Three

TURMOIL IN THE REST OF THE WORLD

How did Canada compare to the world's other nations during the Confederation decades? The answer to that question is essential if one is going to make a judgment on the nature of the country at this stage of its development. The failings and successes of Canadian society cannot sensibly, or fairly, be compared only against modern standards. Understanding the contemporary issues facing the rest of the world serves another valuable purpose, because over the next 150 years, millions of immigrants from around the globe would come to play their part in shaping Canada's modern temperament. For those who do not trace their ancestry in Canada back to the Confederation decades, it's also useful to have a basis of comparison.

Of these regions, European nations were a distant third in influencing Canada during the Confederation decades, well behind Britain and America. In Europe, like the United States during this period, events were much harsher and more disruptive than in Britain or her North American colonies.

For example, during these decades, France endured violent disturbances, ideological conflicts, and major wars. Yet France had little significant impact on Canada, even in her former North American colonies. After 1759, with French Canada ceded to Britain, the flow of French-speaking settlers all but ceased.

Later, when France created her own empire, her colonists migrated to North Africa and Indo-China rather than Canada. As a result, French-speaking Canada remained effectively isolated from the rest of the French world. While French Canada remained relatively tranquil, France was wracked by the French Revolution, the Napoleonic Wars, and the Bourbon Restoration. As a result, French-Canadian culture grew and prospered with a very different character than its European parent.

During the Confederation decades, the revolutionary spirit behind the Revolution of 1848 and the Second French Republic was followed by an anti-democratic Second French Empire under Napoleon III. While there was relative peace in Canada, France fought wars with Russia, Austria, and Prussia. The Second French Empire collapsed after its defeat by Prussia, creating behind it the Third French Republic. And in the final phase of this period, the Third French Republic was domestically more democratic and tranquil, but like the rest of Europe, France was also in a feverish and violent scramble to secure foreign colonies.

Germany, for the initial years of the Confederation decades, consisted of thirty-nine independent realms. It was a time characterized by political manoeuvrings to create a single country, all of it overshadowed by a series of three major wars — with Denmark, Austria, and France. For Germany, like France, the period was a time of rapid economic modernization and violent uprisings. Industrial growth was matched by the demand for democratic reform. The urban poor, students, and the liberal middle classes all appealed for fundamental democratic change. It eventually came, but in fits and starts. These years also saw the beginnings of large-scale migration to the United States.

The Austro-Hungarian Empire, which was created from the amalgamation of the Austrian Empire and the Kingdom of Hungary, was one of the most diverse and important states of this period. Because of the various peoples it ruled, it was in some areas highly industrialized and in others almost feudal. This contiguous European empire had national elements that were Austrian, Hungarian, Polish, Czech, Serb, Ukrainian, Italian, Croatian, Slovenian, Romanian, Bosnian, and Slovakian. It was understandably a convoluted agglomeration that placed competing demands on its complex and inefficient central government.

Russia, a vast empire stretching over two continents — from Poland to the Pacific Ocean and from the Arctic Ocean to Mongolia — was for the most part intensely rural and backward. Russia was a graceless powder keg of an empire with only a few industrialised cities west of the Urals. The Russians lost a war fighting Britain and France in the Crimea, but later had success tearing chunks from the decaying Ottoman Empire and an enfeebled China.

Russia abolished serfdom in 1861. Much like the United States with slavery, this was the most prominent event in Russia's nineteenth-century history. At the time, 37 percent of the population were serfs. Freeing the serfs meant millions of landless people drifted into the cities searching for work. Throughout the Confederation decades, Russia was in serious trouble. She had no sizeable middle class, an oppressive, despotic, and overly centralized government, medieval conditions of poverty, and dozens of angry and alienated ethnic and religious minorities. It was about as different a country from Canada as one could imagine.

Of the major European nations of the era, Italy went through the most unstable period. It was for the most part poor, agricultural, intensely regional in outlook, and riven by a bewildering number of political ideologies. Many of Italy's small constituent states and kingdoms were under foreign or papal rule; and initially, there was no overriding sense of national spirit, such as existed in France or Germany. These decades were a time of shifting loyalties and violent political upheavals. Italians suffered through numerous civil conflicts, frequent insurrections, and major external wars with France and Austria. In the highly fractured south, a state of near anarchy existed for most of the Confederation decades. South of Rome, the period was characterized by widespread lawlessness, large-scale banditry, and rule by large private armies, or "mafie." Italy was eventually unified in 1871, but the new state struggled with unresolved tensions and had dramatic cultural, political, and economic differences between the prosperous urban north and the agricultural south.

Life was somewhat more tranquil for northern Europe's smaller states. Scandinavia enjoyed an era of relative peace, with the exception of Denmark, which lost a war with much more powerful Germany. Norway and Sweden, somewhat like Upper and Lower Canada, remained unified under a Swedish monarchy, but with separate national institutions. To the south, Spain and Portugal were separate countries, having divided in 1840. Spain lost most of its overseas possessions during this period; and beyond their own colonies, both countries exerted little influence in foreign affairs. They both remained poor, non-industrial, and governed by authoritarian regimes.

On the eastern edge of Europe, the Confederation decades witnessed the beginning of the end of Turkey's imperial rule. The Ottoman Empire started the period ruling much of southern Europe, large areas of north Africa and most of what we now call the Middle East. However, sclerotic government in Turkey, growing nationalism and ethnic pride in the peoples of southern Europe and the Arab world, as well as north European imperial expansion all resulted in a series of wars and uprisings coalescing to begin the long decline of Turkey's colonial possessions.

In south Asia, Britain steadily extended and tightened its control over virtually the entire region in a series of small but bloody campaigns, the most important of which was the Indian Mutiny in 1856. The mutiny was ruthlessly supressed, leading to the governance of India passing from the East India Company to the British government, while allowing some form of indirect rule in 175 semi-autonomous "princely states." These years also saw horrific famines in the subcontinent. In total, during this time, over ten million people starved to death.

Not all was bad in India at the time, though. The Confederation decades were also the years which saw the beginnings of the the Bengali Renaissance, a period of intellectual, creative, and social change in Indian society that continues today.

China's history during the Confederation decades was a tale of continuous catastrophe and tragedy. The period was dominated by the fourteen-year-long Taiping Civil War, which saw the bizarrely named Taiping Heavenly Kingdom of Peace fighting to overthrow the Qing Dynasty. Euphemistically called "The Taiping Rebellion" in the West, it was a civil war — one that left a staggering twenty million dead.

Surprisingly, the period was also a time of massive population explosion as China grew to four hundred million people. The entire country, which was supported by a fragile system of subsistence agriculture, was, however, characterized by regular crop failures. During this period, the country suffered from floods, droughts, and famines, all of which took a toll on its population.

At the same time, China had to fight several wars on its borders with European powers and Russians. It was unsuccessful in all of them. China lost its lands north of the Amur river to Russia, while the two Opium Wars and numerous skirmishes with Britain saw the establishment of eighty "Treaty Ports," cities that were in reality colonial possessions of Britain and that allowed it to forcibly open China's markets to the Europeans. The existence of the Treaty Ports had the unintended consequence of accelerating the collapse of the Qing Dynasty.

In the Confederation decades, much of Africa, particularly West Africa, suffered from the long-term damage of the European and Arab slave trades. East Africa had long been open to the outside world, with Portugal controlling much of the coast for the early part of the nineteenth century. In the middle part of the century, the Sultan of Oman seized control of the coast, re-establishing Muslim control. While the coasts had been opened up to outside control, at the outset of the period, by virtue of the continent's geography and climate, most of the interior of Africa had been virtually closed to exploration. This began to change in the 1840s when the major European powers began the scramble to carve out colonies for themselves.

Latin America, before and during this period, had almost no influence on Canada, as the continent struggled to free itself from Spanish and Portuguese domination. For both Africa and Latin America, the Confederation decades were not prosperous times. Most African nations in this period forfeited their natural resources and eventually found themselves left with wildly unstable political systems. South and Central America fared somewhat better. Most achieved independence earlier, but development was glacially slow as many struggled with despotic regimes, border conflicts, and civil wars.

By comparison with the rest of the world, Canada led an enchanted existence during the Confederation decades. Life was insulated and blissfully secure from the problems that assailed the rest of the world. Except for America and Britain, the other nations of the world with all their troubles and calamities could have been on the moon. Canada was almost uniquely fortunate in having a tranquil and relatively peaceful childhood and adolescence. That situation would change abruptly when, a generation later, an angry Serbian student shot the Austrian Archduke, Franz Ferdinand, on a Sarajevo street.

Chapter Four

THE REGIONS AND FIRST PEOPLES: QUEBEC

At the outset of the Confederation decades, Quebec had been in existence as a distinct society for almost two hundred years, as both a French and a British colony. Over this period, it had firmly cemented its own identity, culture, and unique character. For the eight decades preceding 1840, French Quebecers lived a quiet and relatively self-contained life under British rule. French *habitants*, dwelling for the most part on farms and in small villages, had followed a peaceful rural lifestyle with little change to the rhythms of life from one generation to the next. English Quebecers, on the other hand, lived predominately in the colony's two major cities, Quebec City and Montreal, and on farms in the Eastern Townships.

This pattern was about to change substantially during the Confederation decades. Like all other societies in North America and Europe, the Industrial Revolution began reshaping Quebec's economic and social landscape. Over a period of eighty years of British rule in Quebec, a steady stream of British merchants and artisans took up residence in the province's two major cities. Montreal and Quebec had become predominantly English-speaking. However, by 1840, things began changing again. For francophones, the first precursors of change became evident as Quebec began the transformation from a rugged, pastoral society into an emerging industrial one.

By 1840 French Canada had been cut off entirely from France for more than eighty years. Immediately following the "conquest," most of the French merchants and administrative officials had voluntarily returned to France. Apart from the clergy, those francophones who remained behind were mostly farmers, whose fortunes and livelihood were tied to the land. The departure of the merchant class was a momentous act that had far-reaching social, political, and economic consequences

A typical Quebec farm scene in the 1870s.

for the province. With the sudden removal of this vital element of the social hierarchy, francophone commercial life went into a prolonged dormant phase. In the same period as this transformational change, the Quebec Act was passed. It was an unusually generous and far-sighted piece of legislation for its time. It guaranteed French property rights, French civil law, as well as religious and political freedoms. In protecting so many of the existing rights and rules, the Quebec Act also served to help preserve a kind of social status quo. In fact, the combined effect of merchant migration and the Quebec Act was such that the remaining elements of French-Canadian society flourished in a strong, regionally based but essentially rural culture. It was a situation that would remain constant for decades.

At the time, francophones accounted for 75 percent of Quebec's white population, with the relatively new English-speaking population accounting for the rest. French-speaking Quebecers were largely self-contained, self-sufficient, and self-reliant. It was a vigorous, tightly knit, intensely Catholic, traditional farming society, with high birth rates and a family-centred culture. By 1851, the colony's census noted that the ratios remained similar, but the province's urban areas had begun to grow. There were 100,000 people living in Quebec City, 88,000 in Montreal, while 500,000 people lived on farms and a further 88,000 lived in villages.[1]

The Confederation era in Quebec was, however, a time of major demographic change. There was an explosion in the population of the province, which almost tripled in size. Substantial growth in both the English and French populations drove major shifts in the provinces demographic and geographic make-up, and with these changes came the beginnings of internal challenges to Quebec's traditional religious character as well as the first phase in developing a vigorous manufacturing sector. Given that there was virtually no francophone immigration, it was an astonishing increase.

During the Confederation era, Quebec was considerably smaller than the province we know today. Canada East consisted of long strips of farmlands interspersed with small villages running along the shores of the St. Lawrence, the Ottawa, the Saint Maurice, and the Saguenay rivers. The most densely populated rural areas were in and around the Island of Montreal, where almost half of the province's population was clustered. To the south of the St. Lawrence, there were other, more recently developed and settled farming areas in the Eastern Townships, as well as a handful of scattered villages in the Laurentians. The massive tract of lakes and boreal forest in Quebec's section of the Canadian Shield, which currently makes up just over 80 percent of the province's land mass, was not to become a part of the province until the early 1900s.

Economically, Quebec was affected by a major downturn in the fur trade during this period. For two hundred years, this trade had been one of the linchpins of the colony's economy. As a commodity, fur was in serious decline by 1840. Fashions in Europe were changing. There was less demand for the beaver felt that was used in making the ornate hats of the Georgian period. As a result, the fur trade's venerable markets, which had been a major source of revenue since the 1600s, began to shrink. At the same time. Canada's fur trade was also negatively affected by the development of domestic European fur farms and improved manufacturing techniques. Instead of using beaver pelts as the basis for high quality felt, Europe's hat makers began mixing wool with the fur of locally raised rabbits. The changes in fashion and manufacturing techniques were also accompanied by a precipitous drop in the wild populations of beaver and other animals. Decades of relentless trapping had dangerously reduced beaver populations. With plummeting returns from eastern Canadian trap lines, for a brief time much of the fur trade shifted to the West coast. This major change in the fur trade had a far-reaching effect in Quebec, as many men who could not be employed in farming had been employed in the fur trade. With the changing fur markets, many rural Quebecers turned to the timber industry as a source of both full-time employment and seasonal work for farmers.

Farming in Quebec during this era was a hard life. Farms were generally small, subsistence operations of less than a hundred acres. For the most part, there was little specialization, with each farm producing a variety of crops for their own consumption. The most common crops included barley, wheat, rye, peas, turnips, beets, corn, tomatoes, and potatoes. Livestock was almost entirely restricted to domestic consumption and consisted of small numbers of cattle, pigs, and poultry.

Prior to the Confederation decades, the export wheat market for Quebec had largely been overtaken by the produce of the more specialized Upper Canadian farmers. As a result, by the beginning of the period, Lower Canada was regularly importing wheat from Upper Canada. Wheat farming in Quebec had also been hit hard by the twin calamities of the repeal of the Corn Laws and a succession of poor crop yields due to rust, pests, and soil depletion in the early 1840s.

These developments forced Quebec's farmers to change. Over the four decades of the period, Quebec farms began to shift into mixed farming and concentrated on the production of horses, cattle, and pigs, all of which found a booming market in the growing cities of Montreal and Quebec City.

One of the most important social changes during the Confederation decades in Quebec was the abolition of the seigneurial system. The seigneurial system was a system of land tenure devised in the early 1600s as a means of encouraging settlement.

The *seigneur*, or land owner, was usually an influential man who was allocated a large tract of land by the king. Seigneurial farms were usually allocated in long, narrow rectangles along the shores of a major river to make the best use of the waterways as a means of transport. These lots became increasingly narrow as farms were passed down from one generation to the next. A portion of the seigneury would normally be kept by the seigneur and farmed by his family; the rest would be rented out to other habitants. The habitants farmed the land and paid the seigneur a portion of his crops and sometimes a cash tithe. The habitant was also responsible for deforesting the property and erecting houses, barns, and out-buildings.

The seigneur in turn had his own set of responsibilities. He normally served as the local magistrate with authority in matters of civil law and, more often than not, he owned the local mill used by his habitant tenants.

It's important to note that the seigneurial system was not considered harsh or exploitive. Most seigneurs were fair, middle-class landlords who lived and worked locally, and the Canadian habitant was by no means a peasant in the European sense. He was free to live and work where and as he pleased. Despite this, there were problems with this system of land ownership — seigneurially allocated farms routinely stayed within families for generations, and over time, the operation of seigneuries proved to be an impediment to rural commerce, as it prevented farmers from accumulating capital. The seigneurial system also became a casualty of changing economic times in Quebec. Habitant farmers could and did leave their land for better opportunities. Many left when the farmer's seigneurial allocation could no longer be sub-divided as an inheritance. And during times of depressed agricultural markets, thousands left their farms to work in the timber trade, or chose to seek work in Montreal, Quebec City, and the factories of New England.

Unlike farming, where both production and the market tended to be more precarious, timber was relatively low risk and consistently provided solid returns on invested capital. It became Canada's critical foreign export for most of the Confederation decades. This was especially true in Quebec, where timber spurred the growth of Montreal, which in turn initiated and accelerated the demographic shifts from the francophone rural areas to Montreal's newly constructed factories.

The timber trade was one of the nineteenth century's principal engines of economic growth. Timber became a vital Canadian export during the Napoleonic

Ships in Quebec City's harbour load timber destined for Britain in 1869.

Wars as Britain was denied access to Nordic timber. Cut off from her traditional sources for building her naval fleet and domestic construction, Britain turned to Canada. After the wars, healthy markets in Europe and America meant that the timber industry and its supporting services continued to be strong for years after the Confederation decades.

Early in the Confederation decades, there were almost as many people living in Quebec's small rural villages as there were in Montreal — a situation that would change drastically within a century. In the forty years of the Confederation decades, there were just over two hundred villages and hamlets in rural Quebec. Their populations normally ranged from over a hundred to rarely more than two thousand people. Quebec's villages developed in rural areas where churches or mills had been established by seigneurs, usually every eight to twelve kilometres apart. By the 1840s, most of the larger villages had become the economic, social, and religious hubs for their surrounding areas. Typically, they contained a small school, a general store, a blacksmith's shop, an ashery for making soap, a small local brewery, and often a tannery.

Almost every village had at its centre a church, frequently made of stone and surrounded by timber houses and buildings. As in many European countries, several Quebec villages had barns and farm buildings located right in the village. With the exception of the parish priest and the seigneur, both of whom held positions of moral and legal authority in society, most of Quebec's farming villages were egalitarian communities. Some seigneurs lived in the villages, but most were

not conspicuously wealthy. There was no real middle class and, given the self-sufficiency of the larger community, there were relatively few full-time merchants, craftsmen, or hired labourers.[2]

The two most important cities in Quebec during the Confederation decades were Montreal and Quebec City. In the early 1800s, Quebec was the third largest port in North America and the capital of Lower Canada. In the pre-Confederation decades, Quebec City was arguably the most important city in Canada. In addition to its port, its government offices, its timber industry and shipbuilding, Quebec had a military garrison and was the centre of a web of skilled craft workers. By all measures, the "Gibraltar of North America" seemed destined for a grand future.

However, beginning in the 1840s, Quebec City's growth was stymied by the rise of Montreal as the Canadian economy began its first shift from traditional, low-volume, artisanal production to mass manufacturing. Quebec's port would suffer a humiliating loss of business to a much more aggressive and entrepreneurial Montreal Port Authority. And as Montreal grew, she rapidly built modern factories, eclipsing much of Quebec's cottage production. To add injury to insult, by the end of the Confederation decades, Quebec's wooden shipbuilding industry would shrivel as trans-Atlantic fleets converted from wooden sailing ships to steel, steam-powered vessels.

Montreal's rise to prominence and the rapid eclipse of Quebec City as a transportation centre was primarily the result of city planners developing the Lachine Canal, and then several years later dredging the St. Lawrence River.

A street scene, Quebec City, 1870s.

commercial and industrial supremacy. With the deeper shipping channel, large, ocean-going ships could travel upriver and take on freight at Montreal. With its new-found importance as a transportation hub, Montreal began to expand its industrial base.[3]

Montreal's development as a seaport was rapidly followed by the creation of railway links uniting Canada East and Canada West, and shortly thereafter tying Nova Scotia and New Brunswick into its economic circle. With its port and rail links, Montreal quickly became the country's economic and cultural centre of gravity. Confident, prosperous, dynamic, and forward-looking, it developed its own booming and robust business culture. Canadian entrepreneurs from the island city established a host of forward-looking industries: banking, telegraph services, garment and leatherwork manufacture, steel shipbuilding, locomotive construction, distilleries, and large-scale breweries sprouted on the island. By 1871, in the city's wood-, iron-, and steel-based industries alone, Montreal was producing two-thirds of Canada's total manufacturing output.[4] The city wasn't just expanding economically, it was also becoming a centre of learning and culture. In addition to having McGill University, the period also saw the establishment of a second campus of Laval Université* as well as the growth of a vigorous sporting and artistic life. Montreal had clearly become the most energetic and vital city in the country.

It was a clever move. The Lachine Canal was initially built on a small scale as a local bypass for the Lachine Rapids. In the late 1840s, far-sighted members of the Montreal Harbour Commission saw the commercial possibilities of expanding the canal and creating an upstream port closer to the break-bulk point for lumber rafted down the Ottawa and St. Lawrence rivers. Working around the clock whenever the ice was off the river, the Harbour Commission employed two dredge boats using the earliest models of steam-powered bucket scoops. The slurry was transferred by hand to two sludge boats and ferried to shore. Once the new shipping channel was completed in 1854, it spelled the end of Quebec City's

* * *

---

* Montreal's Laval campus was renamed the Université de Montréal after the First World War.

In addition to changes to its industrial and business sectors, there were major demographic changes in Montreal. With employment available in the new industries, thousands of people, mostly rural francophones and Irish immigrants, moved to the city to find work in its newly built factories, shops, and mills. By 1865, Montreal had again undergone a demographic shift to become once more a predominantly French-speaking city.

Throughout the period, Montreal was a busy city — and for the most part a safe and peaceful city. But during the Confederation decades, it was a city rigidly divided by ethnicity and class. English and Scottish Protestants firmly shared most of the top tiers of society with a considerably smaller French-speaking professional and merchant class. The working class was largely, but certainly not exclusively, francophone. Large numbers of the recently arrived Irish-Catholic population struggled to find employment in the city's unskilled labour market, and for many years formed a unique underclass. It would not be until well into the twentieth century that there would be any meaningful social mobility amongst the three groups.

If there was little integration amongst the various European immigrant communities until the twentieth century, there was essentially no opportunity for social mobility for the small aboriginal community living in Quebec City during this period.

Aboriginal peoples in Quebec belong to three traditional language groups. The Inuit live in the Arctic regions surrounding the Hudson Strait and Ungava Bay, and in the woodlands of the more southerly areas are the Algonquin and Iroquoian First Nations.

There have been no serious hostilities between settlers in Quebec and aboriginal peoples for the last 250 years. From the end of the Seven Years War until the end of the Confederation decades, with a few exceptions, most First Nations followed traditional lifestyles, living on unsettled lands to the north of the developed areas of the St. Lawrence Basin and the Eastern Townships. And while the two groups lived separately, large numbers of Quebec's First Nations were actively involved in the fur trade.

One of the key reasons aboriginal communities and white settlers lived peacefully in central Canada was because indigenous peoples generally tended to migrate north and settled away from the areas developed by European immigrants. The other major reason was that in Canada, European settlers and First Nations developed an accommodation with one another based on the Royal Proclamation of 1763.

The Royal Proclamation became one of the most important documents in Canadian history, as it affirmed that aboriginal title to lands has always existed, and that all land was to be considered aboriginal land until it was ceded to the Crown by treaty. This milestone declaration specifically prohibited settlers from laying claim to aboriginal land, unless it had been first purchased by the Crown, and then resold to the settlers by the Crown. This was particularly important because, for the most part, French and English settlers regarded North America as empty lands that could be settled at will. This was an attitude in sharp contrast to that held by aboriginal cultures, where the notion of private property, and the concept of large landholdings belonging to individuals, was completely alien.

The issuing of the Royal Proclamation was a landmark event in government relations with aboriginal peoples, one that has important legal implications today. France, it should be noted, had a similar, but not identical, concept of aboriginal sovereignty in distant unsettled areas, in what was then referred to as "Pays d'en Haut," or "upcountry land," which generally meant those lands beyond the settled French colonies.

If the Royal Proclamation was evidence of an intent by the Crown to respect aboriginal title and aboriginal culture, the overall impact of European settler culture on the aboriginal population was still almost exclusively negative. This impact can be seen in the declining aboriginal population during the period. Providing an exact number of the aboriginal peoples in Quebec during the Confederation era is problematic. Reliably detailed figures were not kept during the four censuses of the period. However, by 1840 it was estimated that there were around twelve thousand aboriginals in both Upper and Lower Canada — which reflected a precipitous decline of over six thousand people since 1791. The drop was almost certainly due to the spread of diseases, particularly smallpox.

Smallpox was the scourge of Canada's nineteenth-century aboriginal peoples. First introduced to North America in 1630, the disease's mortality rates had not lessened two hundred years later. In Europe during the 1800s, smallpox was still a horrific disease, killing over 400,000 people. Inoculation with a cow pox vaccination did not become an accepted medical practice in Europe until the early 1820s. By then, the disease had spread in North America and had had a particularly devastating effect on aboriginal populations, who had no resistance. Not just in Quebec, but right across Canada throughout the Confederation era, smallpox would continue to shatter aboriginal communities, killing untold numbers of people.

When the Indian Act was passed in 1876, most First Nations bands in Quebec were living in long-established remote communities. Consequently, for most bands these lands became their official reserves and they were not forced to move. The Indian Act, amongst other things, established the legal basis for "Indian Reserves," which were defined as land "for the use and benefit of the respective bands for which they were set apart."[5] As an historical aside, Canada's first reservation, "Sillery," was established in 1638 in what is now a part of the Ste-Foy area of Quebec City. The settlement had been set aside as the home for forty Algonquin Christian families, who lived there except for the hunting season. The reserve's status lapsed when it was abandoned due to disease and the subsequent migration of the original inhabitants.

An important aspect to bear in mind concerning the reserves that were established in 1876, one that has current significance, is that reserves should not be confused with land claims areas. Land claims areas do not necessarily relate to any particular reserves, but instead refer to those First Nation lands that were traditionally used for food gathering and were occupied by aboriginal peoples. In this respect, the Royal Proclamation of 1763 imposes an enormous obligation to provide fair compensation and recognition of the possession and tenure of ancient lands. During the Confederation decades, the Royal Proclamation was effectively ignored.

Chapter Five

THE REGIONS AND FIRST PEOPLES: ONTARIO

Ontario's territory grew significantly during the Confederation decades. Canada West initially consisted of the Ottawa River Valley, southern Ontario, and a strip running north of the shores of Lake Huron and Lake Superior. By 1880, the province had expanded westward to the current Manitoba border and northward, although it stopped well short of James Bay. Like Quebec, Ontario did not take possession of its northern regions until the twentieth century.

Unlike Quebec, which had slower economic and demographic growth prior to the Confederation decades but more far-reaching social change, Ontario's growth rate was considerably swifter, more dramatic, and somewhat more predictable. In the early 1840s, Canada West had a population of about 480,000. By the end of the Confederation decades, it had grown by nearly 1.5 million people. This phenomenal increase was due almost entirely to a continuous stream of immigrants arriving from England, Scotland, Ireland, and the United States.

Despite the tidal wave of immigration, by current standards Ontario was not a very diverse province. By the end of the decade, the population would self-identify for the census takers as being: 42 percent Irish, 32 percent English, 24 percent Scottish, and 3 percent Welsh; 159,000 were German, and 75,000 were French. It is worth noting that for census purposes, aboriginal peoples failed to make the list altogether, while the officials who administered the census, perhaps to hide the fact that the province was in danger of being culturally overwhelmed, decided that "American" did not qualify as an option for national origin.

In terms of religious beliefs, Ontarians of the period were overwhelmingly mainstream Christian: 29 percent professed to be Methodist; 22 percent Presbyterian; 20 percent Anglican; 17 percent Catholic; and 5 percent listed themselves as Baptist.[1]

The province's industrial development moved at a pace as brisk as its explosive population growth. Industrial expansion was largely due to the steady improvements to Ontario's transportation systems and its internal communications. The distances that had to be covered when moving goods and the rugged nature of Ontario's forested areas meant that the simplest and most economical means of transportation was via waterways. The St. Lawrence River and the Great Lakes were easily navigable, and throughout the Confederation decades steamships provided ready access to the ports of Montreal and Quebec City. Steamboat travel was well-established by the early years of the Confederation era. The very first steam-powered ships appeared on the St. Lawrence waterways as early as 1816, and by 1840 iron-hulled steamers were running directly from Lake Ontario to Montreal.

The canal systems, so essential to linking major waterways, were based on the ancient First Nations and fur trade portage routes. Initial construction on most canals had been completed prior to 1840. The development of Ontario's canals was closely connected to the lucrative trade in wheat farming. Most Canadian grain was grown in Ontario and getting it to market overseas required canals so that the grain could be shipped from Lake Ontario and Lake Erie to get it to the port of Montreal. This feverish canal construction resulted in almost all of Ontario's major towns being connected by regular, reliable, and relatively cost-effective water links.

Canal construction finally ended in 1848, which conveniently dovetailed with a surge in railway construction. Nonetheless, prior to the completion of what would become a dense network of railway lines in Ontario, steamboats provided the backbone of the province's transportation system. In fact, most of Ontario's principal towns during the Confederation decades were serviced by steamboats with well-appointed dining rooms, salons, and comfortable cabins.

Despite the comfort, steamboat travel on the Great Lakes and the St. Lawrence River was not without its own unique perils. At the time, there were few reliable nautical charts of the Great Lakes system, and in the sudden and violent storms so common on these waterways, groundings and shipwrecks with large-scale loss of life were regular occurrences.

Despite the periodic catastrophes that attended travel by water and the existence of stage coaches, using Ontario's waterways was for years the preferred means of transportation. The province's meagre road system was notoriously awful, and travelling on existing roads, even in good weather, was always problematic. Building roads in Ontario was expensive and the inevitable potholes, flooding, bogs, frost heave, and washed-out culverts that developed once the roads were built meant that they were even costlier to maintain. As a result, the transport of goods, people, and mail relied heavily on steam boats and later railways.

Ontario's rail lines sprouted like spring weeds during the Confederation decades. Early on, they provided fast, efficient linkages between Toronto, Montreal, and Sarnia, as well as connections to American markets.

A Great Lakes steamboat near Toronto, 1860s.

Rail links to the United States were increasingly important, for with the Reciprocity Treaty of 1854, Ontario farmers and merchants vastly increased their trade in grain, lumber, fruit, and manufactured wares to the northern states. By the end of the period, Ontario's network of rail lines would cover a dense web, providing linkages as far west as Sault Ste. Marie, with connections east into Quebec, south to the United States on several crossings, and to all the province's major cities and towns.

Ontario's Confederation-era railways and waterways carried people, lumber, minerals, and a range of manufactured goods; but their most important cargo was the province's agricultural produce.

Trains on the Ottawa–Montreal Line, 1878.

Farming employed the vast majority of the population in Ontario. Farmers, if they weren't tenants, usually owned the land they tilled. Unlike the seigneurial system that was phased out in Quebec, Ontario's farmers operated on the basis of "free and common socage," an ancient and quaint term for the practice of purchasing one's land and having land ownership treated in the eyes of the law as normal personal property.[2] It is unlikely that the system of land ownership had much effect on the agricultural productivity of farmers in either Ontario or Quebec. However, there were significant differences in the profitability of the farms in Ontario and Quebec.

During the first three decades of the period, agriculture was three times as profitable for farmers in Ontario as it was for those in Quebec.[3] This substantial difference was due to a number of reasons. In Ontario, the land itself was more fertile. At the time, modern farming techniques were not in use anywhere in Canada. Practices such as crop rotation and the use of fertilizers would not become common for many years. Thus, Ontario farms had not been subject to the same period of soil exhaustion as had the much older and more extensively tilled Quebec farms. Additionally, Ontario farmers were quicker to move away from subsistence farming. With more diverse and developed transportation links into populous American markets, Ontario farmers could more readily export surplus production to the United States.[4] Accordingly, Ontario farmers took advantage of the greater incentives to specialize in their agricultural production and they began raising high-volume crops for external markets.

The business of farming in Ontario during these years was also slightly more complex than it was in Quebec. In Quebec, at least for the early years of the period, farmers on rented land tended to follow the long-established agricultural practices in use during the seigneurial system. On the other hand, in Ontario during the Confederation decades, landowning farmers were quicker to adopt new machinery and improved processes, and, as a result, agriculture in Ontario developed more rapidly into a complex industry. It is important to note that the distinctions between the two provinces were not the result of innate cultural differences. By 1840, most Western societies had adapted many of the innovations of the Industrial Revolution. In Ontario, by virtue of its more recent origins, there was far greater economic specialization and innovation than had existed when the bulk of Quebec's farmland was opened up. In Ontario, specialization in the agricultural industry had four distinct, associated components.

At the front end of this growing industry was land sales. Land sales and land speculation were highly lucrative businesses for both the government, which allocated undeveloped lands, and the small number of individuals who sold existing farms. Once forested land had been purchased, clearing the land and removing its stumps was essential to make the farm productive. Large-scale stump removal was a major undertaking, and it evolved into its own unique and specialized business (for more on this, see Chapter 13). The third component of this growing industry was actually farming the land itself; and just as in Quebec, 80 percent of Ontarians were farmers. The final component, shipping the harvest to market, was probably the most profitable and capital-intensive function of the agricultural business.[5] Much like the modern farm industry, the Confederation-era farmer found himself to be the least profitable link in the agricultural chain.

Farmers at work in an Ontario farm field, 1860s.

Farming in Ontario, on the small family farms of the period, was a precarious occupation. The main commercial crop was wheat, but wheat was a boom and bust commodity. Fickle markets and uncertain harvests meant farmers had to hedge their investment by planting alternative crops. It was a difficult business, and most Ontario farms survived the lean years as self-sufficient operations, capable of producing enough fruit, vegetables, grain, and livestock to provide for the needs of a large family. However, in years when the crop yield was good, they regularly produced wheat surpluses that could be sold as an export product.

Toronto, early 1850s.

Ontario's towns and cities were in their infancy at the outset of the Confederation decades. In the 1840s, Toronto, which had for years been a sleepy outpost settlement, suddenly began to grow. Its growth was stimulated largely by the bustling steamboat operations that ferried people and goods from Montreal and the numerous towns and villages in between. By the 1850s, the steamboat trade, which was seasonal, was overtaken by the railway boom. Because railways could operate year-round, in winter and summer, in good weather and bad, trainloads of new immigrants could disembark at Toronto's new Grand Trunk Railway station at the corner of Bay and Front Streets. This railway boom, in turn, spawned numerous other industries and related services.

In the four decades of the Confederation era, Toronto's population tripled. The city began the period with only thirty thousand people, but ended with over ninety thousand residents. It wasn't until the following decade that Toronto would experience a truly explosive growth phase, seeing the population double again by 1890.

Toronto was a new kind of colonial city in an expanding British Empire. In 1851, 97 percent of the population claimed their family origins in the United Kingdom, with only a third of them being Canadian-born. By 1871, these numbers had changed. Almost three-quarters of the city remained Protestant and almost everyone's family hailed originally from the British Isles, but after Confederation, a clear majority claimed to be Canadian-born. By contemporary multicultural standards, Confederation-era Toronto was monotonously uniform; but it was, in fact, a highly stratified mix of discrete economic classes, religious sects, and social divisions.

Toronto was much less sophisticated and fashionable in the Confederation era than Montreal. Montreal was larger and older — a more established city, with a larger trade sector, established institutions for the arts and higher education, parks, and links to America and Europe. Montreal had a more cosmopolitan air. But Toronto was certainly not the dull "Hog Town" that many of its modern critics and detractors would love to have the rest of Canada believe. Far from being "Toronto the Good," a placid and staid citadel of Victorian rectitude, Toronto was an energetic and dynamic society with its own sense of colour and a unique set of social problems. For example, throughout the Confederation era, unilingual Toronto, with its two factions of Protestant and Catholic Irish, had far more ethnic and sectarian tension than did Montreal with its French-English divide.

As Toronto transformed industrially and commercially, the city's social structure also changed. Prior to the revolution of 1837, Ontario's leaders were drawn from Upper Canada's tightly knit "Family Compact." The members of the Family Compact were all male and came from the government, the established professions, and the clergy. Although the leadership's gender remained the same, during the Confederation decades the most powerful class of people changed drastically. Particularly in Toronto, a new class of influential leaders arose. The city's most prominent leaders now came from an ascendant commercial-industrial elite. A newly enriched generation, with families such as the Eatons, the Masseys, the Gooderhams, and dozens of lesser-known figures, rose to prominence in the social and business realms. They were largely self-made men who

had achieved success as entrepreneurs, tycoons, and industrialists, and they brought with them a new set of purposeful and enterprising attitudes.

As the stolid colonial city on the frontier gave way to the more bustling and industrialized profit-oriented society, so too grew its middle and working classes. Drawn largely from Protestant English and Scottish immigrants, Toronto's "bourgeoisie" became a relatively well-established and successful group, one that thrived with the city's years of growth, stability, and development. Again, as in Montreal, in Toronto an Irish underclass sprang up from the new wave of impoverished but determined immigrants who arrived in the late 1840s.

However, for the poor, whether they were well-established or newly arrived, there was little in the way of help. Except for a few faith-related charities, social services in Toronto were virtually non-existent and much of the urban working- and under-classes lived in desperate conditions. Unemployment, illness, old-age, and disabilities often meant personal catastrophe for Toronto's urban poor.

Ottawa, which was originally a part of the hunting grounds of the Algonquin First Nations, was first settled by Europeans in the early 1800s as a farming and logging community. By 1840, the original settlement, which was named Bytown after Lieutenant Colonel John By, the British Army engineer who built the Rideau Canal, had grown to three thousand people.

Bytown was originally a lumber town; it served as the principle location to dismantle and rebuild the lumber rafts that were floated down the Ottawa River to get them past the Chaudière Falls. In the earliest years of the Confederation decades, the town's major businesses consisted of one lumber mill, a tannery, two foundries, three breweries, and a distillery. The ratio of breweries and distilleries to other businesses perhaps provides some indication of the town's early character.

By 1845, Bytown's temperament was changing. It could boast a further thirty-eight shops and stores. Its growth was steady, if not spectacular. It became a waypoint for transient loggers, and a network of retail businesses grew up, selling pork, flour, and general supplies to the lumber business. By the end of the 1840s, Bytown's service sector expanded further, and its numerous taverns, gaming houses, and brothels did a thriving trade.[6]

Like so many Canadian towns of the period, Bytown was populated with a mixture of English, French, Scottish, and Irish. With this mix, life in Canada's rough future capital wasn't always placid or peaceful. In Ottawa, much like Toronto, many of the earliest English and French settlers resented the arrival of Irish labourers. There were periodic riots and the town's early years were wracked by simmering low-level sectarian violence.

The gentrification of this rowdy frontier town came through good fortune. The town changed its name to Ottawa in 1855; and in 1857, Queen Victoria, peering at a map, noticed it straddled the borders of Ontario and Quebec — and sat at what was thought to be a militarily safe distance from the United States. With little further ado, she chose it to become the capital of a unified Canada East and Canada West. By 1866, Ottawa had sprouted a handsome new set of Parliament buildings, replete with the latest and most modern construction

innovation — central heating. The bill for the new Parliament and a fine collection of neo-Gothic buildings to house a growing civil service was completed for a grand sum of $625,310. For the next fourteen years, government, railways, and an ever-expanding lumber business helped the city grow. The nation's capital ended the Confederation decades as a small city of just under thirty thousand people.

Other Ontario communities of the period, such as Hamilton, London, and Peterborough, were in their infancy during the Confederation era. Each of these towns had regional importance as centres for local retail, as well as small-scale manufacturing, agriculture, and the lumber trade, respectively. However, for them, economic growth during this period was more gradual than that of Toronto and Ottawa. Growth in most of these cities, which today are classified as mid-sized, would not accelerate until the early and mid-twentieth-century manufacturing booms.

Throughout the Confederation decades, while the cities grew and the farms prospered, governments in Ontario ignored the region's First Nations peoples, administering them under the authority of several different kinds of programs. Virtually all of them were either damaging or inefficient.

During the 1830s, following petitions from several aboriginal groups, a British parliamentary inquiry investigated the status and conditions of aboriginal peoples in Canada. Its report clearly stated "that unregulated frontier expansion was disastrous for Native peoples."[7] At that time, the Colonial Office in London handled aboriginal affairs and made it their practice to manage aboriginal issues on a regional basis. The rationale for this was that they believed policies should be designed to accommodate the local conditions of each colony.

In the 1830s, the Government of Upper Canada toyed with the concept of creating "model villages." These were villages where the First Nations would be allocated land and provided with houses and farm equipment. Several model villages were attempted, but most failed. The failure of these model villages was due to insufficient training being provided to prospective indigenous farmers and the issuing of shoddy and inadequate equipment. The program was finally undermined by the unchecked encroachment of aboriginal lands by white farmers. There were, however, a small number of notable successes. In places like the settlement on the Credit River, First Nations were provided fertile land, state of the art equipment, and, most importantly, sustained, supportive mentoring. This, combined with dynamic aboriginal leadership and an indomitable will to survive, meant that these few reserves became models of successful adaptation to farming life.

In the late 1830s, the lieutenant-governor of Upper Canada, Sir Francis Bond Head, devised a plan to create large reserves on the Manitoulin Island archipelago and on the Bruce Peninsula. Bond Head's rationale for creating these large reserves was not to assimilate the First Nations, as had previously been the case, but rather to isolate them from white society. He believed that previous attempts at assimilation, such as the model village program, had not only been failures, but that they were "the most sinful story recorded in the history of the human race."[8] He believed that contact with European settlers had always been to the detriment of natives and that segregating them would be a "kindness." Bond Head's conclusion was that First Nations were better off living by themselves on remote reserves. When his plan was implemented with a group of Ojibwa, they ended up surrendering millions of acres of rich, arable southern lands for tracts of granite and bog in the Canadian Shield. Agricultural support for the affected groups eventually dried up.

Later, in 1850, Sir Charles Bagot led a commission urging centralized control of aboriginal issues. Bagot's commission, amongst other things, noted that First Nations were not being compensated, as per the Royal Proclamation, for surrendered lands. He made a few elementary recommendations on a range of matters, such as ensuring the proper registration of aboriginal title deeds; he put measures into place so that First Nations would be compensated for timber harvested on their lands; and he set up a system to provide livestock, agricultural implements, seeds, and furniture to the entire tribe to replace the practice of giving band leaders the traditional armfuls of personal presents. Bagot's commission was well-intentioned and resulted in improved legislation that went some way to protecting indigenous peoples. It set aside lands to be used as reserves, provided legal protection from the predations of loggers, and created a system that revitalized the compensation process for surrendered lands. However, Bagot also made the ominous recommendation for the development of residential schools. He envisaged a system where First Nations children, when "isolated from the influence of

A residential school in Ontario, 1860s.

their parents ... would imperceptibly acquire the manners, habits and customs of civilized life."[9]

It was argued that residential schools would provide a progressive and enlightened approach to solving what was believed to be the intractable issue of "civilizing the Indian." Egerton Ryerson is widely and justly acclaimed for his progressive role in developing Ontario's educational institutions. He was also an influential advocate for residential schools. He believed in a school system for First Nations separate from the school systems for whites, one that catered to the unique needs of First Nations. In the absence of any other racist views on his part, and given that the much-stated aim of assimilation was seen to be, at the time, an undisputed benefit to be conferred upon aboriginal peoples, it is possible to see that the residential school system was not developed out of malice. Rather, its creation reflected the authoritarian, insensitive, and arrogant thinking of the time. This, after all, was the age of the work house, public hangings, and survival of the fittest. As with every other initiative involving aboriginal affairs, the views of First Nations were not taken into account, nor was any thought given to just how such schools would be administered or overseen. It was a deeply flawed idea disastrously implemented. Residential schools did not become widespread until the mid-1880s, but the germ of the concept took root in the early days of the Confederation decades.

In 1857, Sir John A. Macdonald sponsored "An Act for the Gradual Civilization of the Indians of the Canadas." The act outlined the process by which First Nations people could become full citizens and given the vote. To do so, the individual had to be male and over the age of twenty-one. He had to be literate in English or French, have "minimal education," and not have any debts. He had to be able to prove he was "of good moral character" and submit to a three-year probationary period. If the individual met all these criteria (measures that were never even remotely contemplated for white people), the tribe was to slice off over fifty acres of arable land from their reserve for the individual's exclusive ownership. Aboriginal leaders wisely saw this as an attempt to destroy their culture and to undermine the integrity of existing reserves. In the end, the

act was a dismal failure as disdainful indigenous men overwhelmingly spurned the program.

In 1860, responsibility for the administration of First Nations passed to Canada from Britain. Prior to this, the Crown had concluded numerous treaties with various aboriginal groups. The effect of these, which covered all of Upper Canada, was the transfer of virtually all the land area of Ontario to the government, in exchange for granting title to a few reserves and the promise of a limited range of goods and services. By 1873, with the expansion of Canada to include not only the original provinces of Ontario, Quebec, Nova Scotia, and New Brunswick, but also the North-West Territories, Manitoba, British Columbia, and Prince Edward Island, Canada's aboriginal population jumped from twenty-three thousand to over one hundred thousand people, while at the same time adding hundreds of new tribal groups.

As a result, the Indian Act was introduced as a means of consolidating and standardizing the government's administrative processes dealing with the country's aboriginal population. As we shall see in Chapter 7, which deals with the Prairies, the Indian Act was written without significant aboriginal input and was never designed to promote fairness or reconciliation. It was written in the spirit of the times with the presumptuous good faith and high-handed assurance of an imperialistic society. As a piece of enduring legislation, it reflected a popular, paternalistic, chauvinist, and impatient Victorian world view, one that sought neither fairness nor reconciliation, but aimed to bring about the rapid assimilation of the aboriginal population.

Chapter Six

THE REGIONS AND FIRST PEOPLES:
THE ATLANTIC PROVINCES

Prior to the Confederation era, the Atlantic provinces had been governed under a number of French and British colonial administrations. The most dramatic change in colonial administration came with the end of the Seven Years War in 1763, when the Treaty of Paris ceded the hardy and self-reliant Acadian colonies in P.E.I. and New Brunswick to Britain. This momentous transition to British rule initiated a pattern of immigration that was to alter the cultural makeup of the Atlantic provinces for more than a century and a half. Under British rule, English, Irish, Scots, Germans, and Americans moved to the region in relatively large numbers, leaving an English-speaking majority with regional enclaves of French-speaking Acadians.

With the exception of Cape Breton, which had for a brief period been an independent colony but rejoined Nova Scotia in 1820, Atlantic Canada's colonial governance structure remained relatively stable. By the outset of the Confederation era, the region was organized along the lines that we are familiar with today.

Nova Scotia, in 1848, became the first of the British North American colonies to achieve responsible government. The colony had a pronounced independent streak, and in the run-up to Confederation there was a stubborn and determined group who, for reasons of regional pride and well-established business connections, bitterly resisted joining the union with Canada. Nova Scotia's traditional trading ties had been, via seaborne trade, with New England and Britain. For a sizeable minority, the concept of throwing their future in with Quebec and Ontario seemed not only counterintuitive and foolish, but economically suicidal. However, the case favouring union with Canada prevailed. The fear of being swallowed up by the Americans persuaded the majority to go along with Confederation. Given the province's recent history, this was an issue with a special pertinence for Nova Scotians, for in the immediate post-Civil War years, many Americans were less than pleased with the fact that Nova Scotia had done a brisk and profitable trade with both the North and the South throughout much of that conflict. There were other reasons favouring union: the Fenian threat, the cancellation of the Reciprocity Treaty with the United States, and the promise of railways linking Nova Scotians to new and growing markets in Ontario and Quebec all played their part in convincing Nova Scotians to join Canada.

The new union also came at a time of declining fortunes in both Nova Scotia and New Brunswick. The two provinces had developed strong lumber trades, which in turn spawned vigorous local shipbuilding industries. By the early 1850s, the shipyards on New Brunswick's rivers were producing a hundred ships a year. By 1875, more than five hundred oceangoing ships were built in Canadian shipyards, most of them in Nova Scotia and New Brunswick. And by the end of the Confederation decades, Canada, with more than seven thousand registered ships, was the fourth largest ship owner in the world.[1] It was a golden age, but it would not last. Technological change would soon make wooden sailing ships obsolete. With tentative beginnings in the early years of the Confederation decades, the world's shipbuilding industry began to modernize. Exploiting the use of copper, iron, and steel composite hulls, this lucrative trade began slowly shifting away from Canada to Northern Ireland, northern England, the Baltic, the Mediterranean, and America's eastern seaboard.

Nova Scotia's decline in shipbuilding overlapped with its development as a coal producing region. Cape Breton shipped coal to Ontario and Quebec via the Intercolonial Railway and by ship, using the recently re-dredged and deepened St. Lawrence shipping channel. Cape Breton coal became a vital commodity in the growth of a newly united country, but the large-scale industrialization that coal supported was of much more benefit to Ontario and Quebec than the Atlantic provinces. Fishing, lumbering, and mining continued to be the economic backbone of both Nova Scotia and New Brunswick.

For much of the Maritimes during the Confederation era, agriculture remained largely at a subsistence level. However, there were exceptions. For example, the Annapolis Valley in Nova Scotia began intensive and profitable farming of apples, finding markets in the other provinces, Britain, and the U.S.A.

Regional farming in Nova Scotia and New Brunswick often supported the lumber industry. The thousands of work horses that worked winter and summer in the provinces' forests consumed immense quantities of hay and oats. Each of the massive Clydesdales, Belgians, Shires, and Percherons that became the logging industry's pride ate literally tons of hay and oats each year. Catering to the draft horse market, many farms that would otherwise have been subsistence operations turned to these basic but profitable cash crops.

Local demand for wheat, which had never been a major cash crop in Nova Scotia or New Brunswick, was virtually eliminated in the Maritimes as the newly built railways brought in cheaper grain and flour from Ontario. For a brief time, P.E.I. struggled on as the

A New Brunswick farm in the late Confederation period.

exception to this set of circumstances. The Island's farmers had had the distinction of being the first from any Maritime province to register an agricultural surplus when they began exporting wheat to Britain as early as 1831. It didn't last, but during the Confederation era, P.E.I. found its niche.

Potatoes, grown in the province's distinctive red soils, had always been an important crop. However, it was during the Confederation era that potatoes steadily became the province's most valuable cash crop. In an export boom that has endured as long as Canada, P.E.I. farmers in increasing numbers specialized in raising potato crops. They began shipping potatoes to every other province, the U.S., and the Caribbean — and in doing so did much to ensure that P.E.I. prospered as a steady, self-reliant, and modestly comfortable rural society.

A cold journey, the most common form of winter transportation before the arrival of the railway.

The Maritimes' two major cities during the era were Halifax and Saint John, New Brunswick. Halifax had a long and colourful history as an important naval base, a function it retains today. The city prospered during the American Civil War. Part of the reason was that Haligonian merchants did a brisk business supplying the wartime needs of the North; at the same time, they provided a sanctuary and a base for the resupply of Confederate blockade runners — which is not to say that most of the population were strong supporters of the South. Since the arrival of freed slaves who fought for the British in Loyalist times, Halifax has had a sizeable black population, and there was virtually no support for the institution of slavery. Most of the population sympathized with the North, and scores of the city's young men who had personal and family links with New England chose to serve in the Union Army.

Halifax's growth was a result of several factors: its importance as a military and naval base, shipbuilding, its status as a colonial and provincial capital city, its deep-water port (mainland North America's closest port to Europe), and the lumber and fishing industries all contributed to its prosperity. However, for some Halifax merchants, Confederation proved to be a disappointment. The growth of heavy industry and manufacturing that had been hoped for failed to materialize, and the railway links to the American ports of Boston and Portland siphoned off much of the anticipated shipping business from Quebec and Ontario.

To the south, on the Fundy Coast, just prior to the Confederation decades, Saint John, New Brunswick, was Canada's third largest city. Originally a bastion of Loyalist Protestants, its character was changed forever with the arrival of large numbers of Scots, followed by Irish fleeing the potato famine. Its status as a port, along with its lumber and shipbuilding industries, had seemed to guarantee it a gilded future. However, it was not to be. Despite slow but steady economic growth from the 1850s to the 1870s, the decline of shipbuilding was the first symptom of looming economic torpor and slow growth. Recovery was dealt a punishing and unforeseen blow when the city's luck turned to disaster in 1877. A warehouse fire spread out of control and, in a nine-hour conflagration, destroyed 40 percent of the town's buildings. Almost all the damage was in the business district.

Because of the city's relatively weak economy, most immigrants who disembarked in Saint John did not stay, but chose to board trains for a more promising future in Ontario and Quebec. To make matters worse, Saint John and New Brunswick experienced a sizeable exodus as many young people moved south to New England in search of steady work and higher paying jobs.

Although Newfoundland shared many characteristics with the other Atlantic provinces, its history and culture differed in many ways. Throughout the Confederation era, and for several decades after, Newfoundlanders did not identify with mainland Canadians. They saw themselves as an inextricable part of a British North Atlantic community and regarded all of North America as being politically and culturally foreign. In addition to this idiosyncratic attachment to the old country, most Newfoundlanders had a passionate sense of their own identity, and had no intention of diluting their identity or traditions with those of mainland Canada. This wasn't a reaction to pressure to join Confederation. Newfoundland's unique sense of self was firmly established. As early as 1840, it was the only colony to create its own national flag.

Regardless of Newfoundland's distinctive character, its population was still deeply divided, with communities split along sectarian lines. Notwithstanding some valiant attempts by politicians to bridge the rift between the various communities, English and Irish Newfoundlanders for the most part viewed one another with deep distrust, and Protestants and Catholics remained fervidly split into two guarded and uneasy communities.

Intercommunal suspicion and hostility invariably distorts any society's collective common sense. Newfoundland was no exception. In the mid-nineteenth century, the island's sectarian split made for bizarre politics. Politicians campaigning in the 1850s argued that responsible government would be a disaster for Newfoundland, because it would ultimately give control of the legislature to the Roman Catholics. A few years later, many of Newfoundland's Irish Roman Catholics fought equally as spiritedly, and more successfully, against union with Canada, on the grounds that Irish Catholics had already gained home rule in Newfoundland. Why would they ever want to risk losing it by uniting with Ontario, which everyone could see was a nest of anti-Catholic bigotry. In the old country, union had been a devastating experience; why would any sane person ever want to repeat this catastrophe?

Fortunately, with the passage of time and a more tolerant social disposition, virtually all the acrimony and suspicion between the various factions in Newfoundland has long since disappeared. And while it is true that bigoted attitudes flourish in isolated circumstances, other more positive attributes do as well. In Newfoundland's case, many of these qualities survive today as characteristic features of the province's people. Hardiness, generosity, warmth, endurance, and a cheerful, open disposition were all molded through decades of privation and peril in the island's small outport communities.

Those positive Newfoundland traits were rooted in a difficult lifestyle. Life in the outports in mid-nineteenth-century Newfoundland was a hard grind. It created a people who had to be mentally tough and resilient if they were to survive. Illnesses from malnutrition were common, and the mortality rate from disease and work-related accidents was high. The fishing and sealing industries employed close to 90 percent of the population; and most of the colony's 162,000 people lived in small, isolated fishing communities perched on the edges of Newfoundland's bays and anchorages.

Contemporary accounts of Newfoundland's outports invariably described similar scenes. Each village was generally located on a small harbour, most often with one or two schooners and numerous fishing boats riding at anchor. On the wooden quayside would be a few unpainted sheds draped with fishnets laid out to dry. Close to the dock were rows of fish flakes, and frameworks of poles and boughs covered in drying cod. Higher up on the rocks and grass-tufted slopes were square, two-storey wooden houses, and beside each was a scrupulously cultivated patch of kitchen garden, planted with cabbages and root crops to provide variety and nourishment for diets that were all too often deprived of essential nutrients. Newfoundland, with very little good farmland, had virtually no market farming, and costly agricultural imports came mainly from Britain and the United States. Trade with the rest of British North America was minimal.

Seasonal migration was a feature of outport life. In the spring and autumn, Newfoundland men regularly moved inland to cut wood and hunt caribou. In the summers, when the North Atlantic was relatively calm, they went to sea — most often in sixteen-foot open dories for the inshore fishery, or in twenty-five-foot schooner-rigged jack boats when they fished the outer headland waters. In the winter, life took a more hazardous turn when men from the outports moved in large numbers out onto the ice floes to hunt harp seals. It was a gruelling existence.

Drying and stacking codfish in a Newfoundland outport village, 1880.

St. John's was the only Newfoundland town of any size during the Confederation decades. During this period, its population tripled in size, growing from just over ten thousand people to thirty thousand. One observer described the capital at the outset of the period as being made up of:

> Large stone houses, good-sized churches, chapels, and court-houses: shops built of wood and painted white, a tolerably regular street, and a road or two, mark the seat of greater wealth, and a more numerous population. Even in St. John's however fish flakes are by no means entirely absent, though they are confined to the south side of the harbour and to a small nook bearing the euphonious appellation of Maggoty Cove.[2]

Just as life was never easy for outport villagers, St. John's had more than its share of disasters. The city was destroyed by fires five times during the nineteenth century. Confederation era Newfoundlanders suffered more than their share of tragedy and hardship. But if life was hard for the descendants of the island's European settlers, it was considerably worse for the indigenous population.

Except for the Beothuk in Newfoundland, the experience of aboriginal Canadians in Atlantic Canada was in many ways similar to First Nations in Ontario.

Little is known of the original indigenous people of Newfoundland, the Beothuk. They were believed to be an Algonquin-speaking people, who numbered somewhere between five hundred and two thousand people at the time of major European contact. The Beothuk were declared extinct as a people in 1829, as a result of starvation, disease, and conflict with white settlers and Mi'kmaq First Nation populations. With the arrival of white settlers, the Beothuk had moved inland, away from their traditional lands where they hunted for seal and caribou. Inland, their numbers fell drastically — a result of the combined effects of losing their original hunting areas and the effects of disease on the population's hunting-age males.

By the beginning of the Confederation decades, Newfoundland's remaining aboriginal peoples were Mi'kmaq. Whether or not the Mi'kmaq were native to Newfoundland or not is a contentious issue. Some argue they came to Newfoundland from Cape Breton after the first white settlements; others claim they were living in Newfoundland alongside the Beothuks centuries before. However, by the 1830s, there were believed to be several hundred Mi'kmaq living on the island. With the extinction of the Beothuks, Mi'kmaq bands moved from the southern areas of Newfoundland and into the interior of the island, where they followed a relatively undisturbed and traditional way of life until the very late nineteenth century, when the arrival of railways brought white hunters and settlements into Newfoundland's interior.

In Labrador, there are three aboriginal groups: the Innu, the Inuit, and the Southern Inuit. The Innu are a part of the Algonquian-language group of peoples and one of Labrador's two pre-contact aboriginal peoples. The Inuit are an indigenous people who are believed to have migrated from the sub-Arctic south along the coast to Labrador almost eight centuries ago. The Southern Inuit, similar to the Métis elsewhere in Canada, have mixed aboriginal-white ancestry. Descended from Europeans, primarily English fishermen, and Labrador Inuit, they differ significantly from the Inuit and have their own distinctive culture.

The Innu people have historically lived in the boreal forests of Labrador. They speak a dialect similar to Eastern Cree; and until the arrival of the Hudson's Bay Company in 1830, they followed a traditional nomadic hunter-gatherer existence. In the late eighteenth century, with the assistance of Moravian missionaries, many of the Innu converted to Christianity. However, it was the arrival of the fur trade that had the most disruptive effect on the Innu. As they adapted to the benefits of this new economy, they ceased being nomadic caribou hunters and moved to more permanent village locations. Instead of a nomadic hunting life, they primarily manned trap lines and hunted and fished locally. For many, it was a ruinous change to their lifestyle, as the more permanent settlements often faced periods of famine — the result of depletion of their food sources through over-hunting. Their migration also subsequently meant that because they were relatively recent migrants, in the law's eyes, they were not entitled to aboriginal land settlements. Like all aboriginal peoples, the Innu suffered heavily from introduced diseases.

The Inuit in Labrador had the longest contact with Europeans, with trading first recorded between Labrador Inuit and sixteenth-century Basque whale hunters. By the time of the Confederation decades, the Inuit had become Christians, again through the ministry of Moravian missionaries. Their traditional lifestyle evolved, largely as a result of their contact with European trade networks and the frequent visits of whaling ships.

Beginning in the late eighteenth century and continuing throughout the nineteenth century, along the south coast of Labrador, European fishermen and whalers took Inuit wives and settled along Labrador's southern coast. By the outset of the Confederation decades, the resulting mixed "Southern Inuit" culture was well-established and displayed many unique cultural dissimilarities from the more northerly Inuit. Although the Southern Inuit have been variously called "Southern Inuit Métis," or "Labrador Métis," they are an entirely separate and distinct culture from the Métis found in western Canada.

In the Maritime provinces, various Mi'kmaq and Maliseet tribes made up the largest element of the First Nations populations. Their territories stretched from the south shore of the Gaspé through New Brunswick, Nova Scotia, and Prince Edward Island. Both the Mi'kmaq and Maliseet people belong to a larger linguistic and tribal grouping known as the Wabanaki Confederacy, which extends well into the United States.

As a result of considerable inter-marriage, the two tribes were initially allied with the French. They both made peace with the British after the Seven Years War. However, because the Royal Proclamation of 1763 made no mention of any of the Maritime colonies, Loyalist settlers assumed that the Maritimes were empty spaces and largely ignored their land rights. Much the same pattern of development followed as in Quebec and in Ontario, with the advance of white agricultural settlements forcing aboriginal migration.

As farming communities developed, nomadic First Nations were squeezed off their traditional hunting grounds, moving to re-establish themselves in more remote and less valuable areas. In all three Maritime provinces, there were attempts to establish First Nations as farmers. However, just as in Ontario, these programs failed — for similar reasons. The programs themselves were badly conceived and ineffectively run. They were insufficiently resourced in terms of training and equipment, and, most distressingly for the unschooled First Nations bands, white farmers were allowed to clear and farm reserved lands that had never been properly documented.

Throughout the Confederation decades, First Nations in the Atlantic provinces were gradually and inexorably thrust onto the margins of white society, eking out their lives hunting and fishing, and finding occasional seasonal employment in the lumber trade, in the inshore fisheries, and later as labourers on the railways.

Chapter Seven

THE REGIONS AND FIRST PEOPLES:
THE WEST AND THE NORTH

Large-scale European settlement of the West took place after the Confederation decades; accordingly, the narrative of the West in this period is a story of small numbers.

By the 1840s, Manitoba had just over six thousand people, the majority of whom were Métis, a community that had been established in the area for over a century. The single largest minority population consisted of Scots living in the "Red River Colony," which had been formed as a humanitarian project by Lord Selkirk in 1812. Selkirk, a Scottish aristocrat, was deeply troubled by the forced removal of farmers who were evicted from their small farms to make way for sheep enclosures during the Highland Clearances of the early nineteenth century. The Hudson's Bay Company granted Selkirk a massive tract of 116,000 square miles for his settlement. It was not an act of charity. The company tied three expectations to the land grant: Selkirk's colonists could not compete in the fur trade; the settlers had to provide two hundred men each year for employment with the company; and the colony had to furnish stocks of meat, flour, butter, and vegetables in order to reduce the company's shipping costs of supplies from Britain. Selkirk's settlement, in the area that would later become Winnipeg, was the only major settlement that the Hudson's Bay Company established in its 1.5 million-acre territory.[1]

Long before the arrival of the Red River settlers, the Métis were well-established. Métis communities and an independent Métis culture had been in existence and growing in southern Manitoba since the days of the early French fur trade, when fur traders married and co-habitated with First Nations women. At the time of the establishment of Selkirk's settlement, Métis society in southern Manitoba was based on fur trading, hunting, and farming. It was a unique society, partly

Salteaux Métis family, 1860s.

nomadic, following and hunting the buffalo herds, and partly settled and agrarian. Many Métis farmers lived in small hamlets and on strip farms built along the banks of the Red and Assiniboine rivers. The collision of the two cultures marked the beginning of a long period of conflict between the Métis, the Hudson's Bay Company, and, later, the government of Canada.

In the early decades of the century, the Hudson's Bay Company tried to control the fur trade by attempting to restrict the Métis from doing business with their rivals, the North West Company. This heavy-handed constraint quickly led to fighting in the short lived "Pemmican War," when a preventable confrontation between Hudson's Bay employees and Métis traders working for the rival North West Company turned violent. At what was called the Battle of Seven Oaks, the Métis fended off an assault by men from the Hudson's Bay Company. In doing so, they killed twenty Hudson's Bay men, including the regional governor, and lost one of their own. Criminal charges were eventually brought against several Métis leaders in British courts, but all were acquitted. It was an ominous series of events, which poisoned relations between the two communities long afterward.

The pace of settlement in Manitoba was slow from the 1840s through to the 1870s. In Canada, the most desirable location to settle was, until then, Ontario. Nonetheless, central Canadians and the British government were not indifferent to the West. The problem they had was that not much was really known about western Canada. Rupert's Land, as it was known then, was a vast area, and few people outside fur traders and First Nations knew what kind of plants and what range of animals lived there — or if the area was even suitable for agriculture. Transportation was also an issue and no one knew precisely where railways could be built.

All of this meant that development of the West was slow; however, the same was not true south of the border. What was worrying to the imperial government was that the Americans were already mapping and charting their western frontier, and were talking seriously about building a railway to the coast. It was feared that in the absence of any solid information about the West, the Americans might well lay claim to it.

In the spirit of intrepid amateurism, the Royal Geographical Society received a grant of £5000 from the government and duly commissioned Captain John Palliser, an army officer and gentleman adventurer, to launch an expedition to explore western Canada. Captain Palliser put together a team of geographers, surveyors, botanists, voyageurs, and hunters, and between 1857 and 1860 they mapped, studied, and reconnoitred much of the Prairies, surveying possible railway routes through the Rocky Mountains. They didn't find a route through the Rockies to the Pacific, but they did vastly add to the geographical and scientific understanding of western Canada. Included amongst Palliser's numerous findings were such things as: the discovery of a fertile belt in the Prairies suitable for farming and cultivation; the clear conclusion that something had to be done to help the native people of the Plains once the buffalo were hunted into extinction; and, the recognition that putting a railway through to the Pacific might be possible, but it would be prohibitively expensive.

At the same time as Palliser's team was surveying the West, another small group of men, interested in securing the West for Canada, had moved to the Prairies and settled in the Red River area. These men established what they called "the Canadian Party." Despite the name, it was less of a political party and more of an obnoxious Canadian lobby group, formed mostly from Orangemen, frontier thugs, and eager land speculators. The Canadian Party made no secret of the fact that it wanted Manitoba to join Canada as a thoroughly English-speaking Protestant province, which was not at all reassuring to the French-speaking Métis.

Back in Ottawa, the Canadian government had plans for the West. John A. Macdonald harboured a vision of a country running "from sea to sea." In addition to the prime minister's grand plan, he was anxious to prevent the Americans from getting there first and laying claim to the Prairies. Macdonald moved quickly to prepare the groundwork for his expansion. In 1868, the Canadian government managed to get the British

Parliament to authorize, for the following year, the transfer of the rights to Rupert's Land from the Hudson's Bay Company to the new Dominion. It was a bargain of historic proportions. Most of western Canada went to the new government for £300,000. It was also an alarming development for the Métis, as they had no part whatsoever in the consultations.

Recognizing that inclusion in a Canadian federation was all but inevitable, the Métis, under the leadership of Louis Riel, set up their own provisional government with the intent of negotiating the region's terms of entry into Confederation. The Red River government had no legal status. Instead, it was a brash measure that Riel hoped would give him some leverage to negotiate the status of the new province. Riel was keen to preserve Métis land rights and French language rights, as well as to secure a commitment for a government-supported Roman Catholic education system, much like the one existing in Quebec. However, things soon went awry.

In 1869, Louis Riel's men arrested Thomas Scott, along with forty-eight other members of the Canadian Party. When they were arrested, Scott and his fellow "Canadians" were readying themselves to storm Upper Fort Garry in an attempt to overthrow the provisional government. Riel actually sentenced Scott's leader, Charles Boulton, to death, but then in an act of magnanimity promptly pardoned him. Things were different for the ill-starred Thomas Scott. He was a loutish, hot-tempered, and insufferable man, who proved to be a truculent and unco-operative prisoner. Riel, offended by Scott's rude behaviour, and acting upon no authority but his own mulish instincts, sentenced Thomas Scott

to death. On March 4, 1870, Scott was dragged in front of a firing squad and executed — the charges were for insubordinate and insulting behaviour.

Scott's death caused a furor in Ontario. Newspapers were filled with lurid and often contradictory accounts of his murder. Sir John A. Macdonald, never one to forgo the opportunity afforded by a crisis, moved quickly. He dispatched troops to the Red River colony, and by May 12, his bill, the Manitoba Act, became law. The Manitoba Act created a new, fifth Canadian province. Relatively small, it was roughly one-eighteenth the size of the current Manitoba.* Four months later, after an exhausting march across Canada (a faster route, going by rail through the United States, was not an option), a column of British regulars and Canadian militia neared Red River. Warned of their approach, Riel fled into exile in the United States.

Riel's efforts hadn't been in vain. Anxious to keep the peace in the new province, Macdonald's new Manitoba Act recognized Métis land rights, English- and French-language rights, as well as Protestant and Roman Catholic educational rights.

However, once Manitoba became a part of Canada, Métis land rights were largely ignored; and by the late 1880s, a movement to retract language and educational rights from French Manitobans would explode as a divisive and ugly national political crisis. By this time, many of the Métis had already left Manitoba. Following the diminishing herds of buffalo, many of the Métis moved away from the Red River to live in unsettled

---

* Manitoba's size would increase in 1886 and again in 1912.

areas in Saskatchewan and Alberta, in what was then the North-West Territories.

Throughout the 1870s, immigration levels in the West were disappointing. Canada went into a steep recession in 1873 and the waves of settlers from abroad that the government hoped for didn't materialize. Instead, most of the migrants to Manitoba in the 1870s came from Ontario. They joined smaller numbers of French-speaking Quebeckers who moved West for the promise of free land. Although there was some limited immigration of Icelanders, German Mennonites, and Central Europeans in this period, it would not be until well into the 1880s that the Prairies saw large-scale European settlement.

For what immigration there was to the West, the chief attraction was free land. For a registration fee of ten dollars, the Dominion Land Act of 1872 gave homesteaders 160 acres of land, with the condition that they had to grow their own crops and live on the land for three years. In theory it sounded like a simple proposition; in practice it was a test of character. Travelling to your new homestead was a daunting effort. Before the railways, if you were coming from overseas, the journey involved a long ocean voyage, almost always crammed below decks in steerage accommodation, followed by a trip by steamer and railway, usually through the United States, and then a long journey by oxcart or on foot to your homestead. At this point, the early settlers' difficulties were just beginning.

The first few years of farming the land were not for the faint of heart. The Prairies had few building materials for house or barn construction, and most settlers had to face Prairie winters living in an uninsulated sod hut for weeks on end with temperatures regularly hovering at -30°C. The weather wasn't the only problem. Growing and raising sufficient food to last through to the next harvest was no simple task. This was especially true for city-raised people who had little experience of farming. In those early years of Prairie settlement, before the railways, 40 percent of homesteaders had to make the heartbreaking decision to give up their dream and abandon their land within the first three years.[2] Given the nature of the problems a settler had to overcome simply to survive for three years, this is an astonishing figure. Sixty percent of those who made it to their homestead managed to keep their 160 acres and went on to develop profitable farms. The high completion rate was a measure of the character of the times. It indicates an unshakeable tenacity and sense of purpose and commitment that is rarely ever required of modern Canadians.

In settling the West, migration was closely tied to railway development. Once railways were introduced to an area, things changed drastically for Prairie farmers. Goods of every conceivable nature could be brought in cheaply and efficiently. Hardware, building supplies, machine tools, and consumer goods of every possible description became available to Prairie pioneers after the introduction of railways.

It was not until December 1878, however, that the first western Canadian railway line was completed. The Pembina Branch, a line of track one hundred kilometres long, ran from St. Boniface to the American border and connected Manitoba to eastern Canada using American railways. The line was initially envisaged in the 1860s, but for political and financial reasons it was not built for nearly two decades. There was no direct Canadian link to the Winnipeg area until 1883.

Manitoba wasn't entirely isolated before its first railway, though. Again, shrewd managers in the Hudson's Bay Company in 1858 searching for ways of reducing logistical costs funded the development of American steamboat companies linking the Red River Colony with Minnesota. The result of these investments meant that steamboats on the Red River throughout the 1860s and '70s rivalled in size and cargo capacity any of those in service on the Mississippi or Missouri rivers.

During the Confederation decades, Alberta and Saskatchewan were a part of the North-West Territories. They became provisional districts in 1882, and were eventually given provincial status in 1905.

At the outset of the era, the two provinces were populated primarily by First Nations tribal groups. Some historians have referred to the early and mid-century period as being a golden period for Plains First Nations. In hindsight, this is almost certainly wrong. The period was more likely a decades-long phase of transition between domestication of the horse and the catastrophic societal collapse that followed European settlement.

In the early decades of the eighteenth century, the first harbinger of European contact on the Canadian Prairies was the arrival of wild horses. Plains First Nations in Canada were quick to adapt to the horse's arrival, and by the Confederation era, horses had been an integral part of their lifestyle for over a century.[3]

The horse changed First Nations societies in positive and negative ways. Mounted bison hunters were able to provide their bands a more abundant and reliable source of food. The horse's domestication made tribes more mobile, allowing them to more readily follow the bison herds, and to own and move a greater number of goods. This new mobility also produced more conflict in the form of horse raids and inter-tribal war.[4] But, most tellingly, the advent of the horse was also the early harbinger of a tidal wave of European migration, which for Plains First Nations was an historical disaster of near immeasurable proportions.

This momentous historical event arguably had a much more negative impact on Plains First Nations than other Canadian aboriginal peoples. Changes to their lifestyle were much more rapid and far-reaching than had been the case for First Nations of the Eastern woodlands or those west and north of Alberta. In the course of four short decades, the spread of disease, the elimination of the bison, and the physical marginalization of First Nations on the Prairies rapidly and irrevocably changed distinctive, functioning cultures into displaced, impoverished, and starving bands of refugees.

The first regular interaction Plains First Nations had with Europeans came in the eighteenth century when French fur traders expanded their operations as far west as the Rocky Mountains. Shortly thereafter, large-scale outbreaks of smallpox on the Prairies were recorded in the 1730s. Smallpox had already devastated Eastern tribes for decades, and as the fur trade pushed west, so too did this deadly pathogen. Records of these first plagues are anecdotal and no one knows for sure how many died, but we do know that it radically changed tribal demographics in many areas of the Prairies.

At around the same time, the arrival of the horse hastened the spread of the disease from a different direction. Smallpox epidemics, which had originated far to the south in the days of the Spanish conquistadores, steadily spread north, eventually arriving on the Canadian Prairies from the territories of more southerly equestrian tribes, such as the Dakotas, Pawnee, Comanche, and Shohsone. These more southerly tribes had already been carrying the infection, and horse trading, wars, and raids inexorably spread the disease to the Canadian Prairies. From this time on, the disease was rampant, recurrently springing up and decimating populations and changing the regional balance of power between tribal groups. Smallpox was not the only disease to produce incalculable damage and misery on Plains First Nations. Just as elsewhere, Europeans brought with them other virulent micro-organisms for which native populations had no resistance. Whooping cough, influenza, measles, scarlet fever, chicken pox, typhoid fever, tuberculosis, and other diseases also spread rapidly over the same period, killing untold numbers of First Nations.[5]

Aboriginal societies on the Prairies suffered a second deadly blow as overhunting the bison across North America reduced their numbers from an estimated pre-1800 population of sixty million to near extinction levels by the mid-1880s. The decline of the bison herds was not a gradual process either. This kind of change followed a characteristic hockey stick curve, with a gradual upturn from 1800 to 1860, and, in Canada, an

A Blackfoot family on the Prairies in the early 1880s. With the bison herds gone, Plains Indians found themselves hungry and displaced in a land that had previously provided them with all their needs.

abrupt increase in the slaughter occurring in the 1870s and 1880s. As early as 1869, the Métis in Manitoba realized the bison herds were in decline, and many of them moved west from Manitoba to settle in Saskatchewan and Alberta, only to have the herds virtually disappear within fifteen years.

The spread of cattle ranching in North America also infected bison with foreign diseases for which they also had little resistance: bovine tuberculosis, tick fever, brucellosis, and anthrax played a secondary role in destroying the bison herds. And if this was not enough, El Niño weather patterns in the 1870s caused years of severe droughts with enormous accompanying grass fires across

Métis buffalo hunters employed in a Canadian survey party, Saskatchewan, 1871. Within five years, the bison and their way of life would be gone forever.

the Prairies — an event that also hastened the collapse of the remaining herds. It almost seemed as if the environment itself was trying to speed the bison's destruction.

Decimated and weakened by disease, with their traditional food sources eliminated, the Plains First Nations were as devastated and tragic a displaced people as any in history. They were left with no place to go and no relief. The vast grasslands could provide no haven.

Native Americans on the plains had suffered the same diseases and lost their bison herds several years earlier. In addition, the U.S. government had, since the early 1860s, been waging a series of calamitous "Indian Wars," wars that left aboriginal peoples not only destitute but utterly defeated. During that final horrendous decade, which saw the destruction of Canada's Plains aboriginal society, criminal whisky traders, settlers, and railway and government officials would inflict even more misery and damage.

Prior to the advent of the railways, American fur traders and criminal frontiersmen established trading posts within the North-West Territories. Although some legitimate trade took place at many of these posts, so too did the unscrupulous practice of selling doubly distilled alcohol to vulnerable populations. Since the earliest days of New France, the fur trade had been associated with the ruinous custom of selling liquor to susceptible aboriginals. There were ineffective attempts to stop this as early as the eighteenth century. Quebec bishops threatened whisky traders with excommunication, and for nearly two hundred years there were other unsuccessful attempts to halt this practice. In the 1870s, in the North-West Territories, unprincipled whisky-traders — like drug dealers a century later — laced their addictive product with a variety of substances. Many frontier traders cut their cheap whisky with deadly substances: sulphuric acid, turpentine, gunpowder, strychnine, pesticides, tobacco, and hot peppers were all mixed into the liquor. In addition, traders in a dozen forts across the North-West Territories regularly cheated the natives of their furs and their horses, and many did a brisk trade in prostituting the starving wives and children of destitute tribes.[6]

One of the worst incidents of frontier lawlessness involved the 1873 killing in southern Saskatchewan of twenty-three natives by a group of drunken American and Canadian whisky traders who were searching for stolen horses. The incident became known as the Cypress Hills Massacre.

To curb growing lawlessness in the West, and to prevent a repetition of the Indian Wars that had taken place in the United States, the government created the North-West Mounted Police. Canada had few local police forces, and at the time, under the British North America Act, law enforcement was entirely a provincial matter. Policing had generally been the responsibility of the courts, but in times of civil emergency, the army was called out. The North-West Mounted Police were originally to be modelled after the Royal Irish Constabulary, but their training, discipline, uniforms, equipment, and organization more closely resembled that of a contemporary light cavalry regiment.

The new police force was spectacularly successful in bringing order to the North-West Territories. Their work was all the more remarkable, considering that they were operating over a vast territory, and, until 1885, had fewer than five hundred members. Operating in small detachments and using the principle of minimum force, the mounted police promptly cleared up the problem of whisky traders, and, in doing so, established close and respectful relations with First Nations.*

---

* The legacy of the North-West Mounted Police had other unintended offshoots. Frequently, their outposts developed into modern Canadian cities, as in the case of Calgary. The detachment's original egocentric and unpopular commander, a Captain Éphrem Brisebois, named the station "Fort Brisebois." The day Brisebois was posted out, the troops renamed their base "Fort Calgary," after Calgary Bay on the Isle of Mull in Scotland. The new name stuck.

Soon after, they became a key player in supervising and stage-managing the signing of what came to be known as the "Numbered Treaties."

The government signed seven numbered treaties (1871–77) with Prairie First Nations during the Confederation decades. (There would eventually be eleven treaties, but four of these were signed after 1889.) Devised in Ottawa, the Numbered Treaties remain a contentious and, in the eyes of many, an ignominious issue in Canadian history — perhaps not so much for what they promised, but for the mendacious and cruel ways in which the government implemented them.

With the buffalo close to extinction, between 1876 and 1878, Canadian Indian agents, acting on instructions from the government in Ottawa, deliberately denied food to starving bands of First Nations. The policy of withholding food until the natives had moved onto designated reserves was an integral part of the enactment of the Numbered Treaties and was intended to do three things: to clear the Prairies of nomadic aboriginal bands, thereby allowing for European farm settlement; to ensure that the construction of the Canadian Pacific Railway progressed unimpeded; and to once and for all destroy the aboriginal people's migratory way of life as a first step in assimilating them into the larger Canadian population. It was a shameful and inexcusable chapter in Canadian history, one that, in the Prairies, inculcated a tradition and an enforced relationship of dependency and neglect.[7] There are no accurate records as to how many people died of starvation as a result of this policy, but the policies of engineered famines and brutally inefficient administration meant that across the Prairies hundreds of First Nations people died of hunger and famine-induced diseases.

On the Prairies, the government promised First Nations reserve lands, hunting and fishing rights, an initial settlement followed by annual payments, as well as assistance with education, health care, and the purchase of agricultural machinery. The Numbered Treaties, along with The Indian Act (1876), became the defining legal instruments in determining the country's ongoing relationship with its aboriginal peoples. In hindsight, it is clear the key expectation underlying the Numbered Treaties was that aboriginal peoples would, in the vocabulary of the period, become "civilized" or assimilated into white society.

Far from assimilating aboriginal Canadians, the Numbered Treaties and the Indian Act provided the historic basis for marginalizing, segregating, and impoverishing them. Although in fairness, despite the prevalent attitudes of the time being decidedly racist and chauvinistic, the impetus behind the Indian Act and the Numbered Treaties was not based upon racial hatred or contempt. As wrong and arrogant as it was, it is important to note that the underlying assumption was that the government thought it was doing the First Nations a huge service by setting up a system that would eventually see aboriginal peoples absorbed into the larger society. Given the establishment of segregated reserves and the prevailing attitudes toward race and social opportunity, this was a hopelessly unworkable contradiction.

Although it was never openly spelled out, reserves were not intended to be permanent homelands, because it was assumed that the aboriginal population would "civilize" and disappear as a cohesive ethnic group. What happened instead was that once First Nations were confined to remote reserves, a rapid and vicious process of institutional seclusion and marginalization began. Physically shunted beyond the margins of society, First Nations could not possibly be assimilated, or even fairly integrated, into the mainstream economy. Denied the vote and forcibly made wards of the state, aboriginal peoples were left with no political influence. Things were made worse as their affairs were overseen by a largely indifferent, tight-fisted, unresponsive, and incompetent government administration. Once First Nations were out of sight on reserves, they were effectively out of mind, and their problems were left to fester.

British Columbia's aboriginal peoples fared only marginally better than the Plains First Nations. European contact resulted in very similar plagues of smallpox and other diseases. Smallpox epidemics erupted with generational regularity on the West Coast. Large-scale epidemics took place in 1770, 1801, 1836, 1853, and 1862. Again, it is impossible to know the precise numbers that died from the disease, but anecdotal records indicate that the disease was ruinous. In the 1862 epidemic alone, almost one-third of the First Nations population on the B.C. coast was believed to have died from the disease. The population of B.C.'s aboriginal peoples plunged from an estimated mid-eighteenth-century level of 180,000 to a late-nineteenth-century low of 35,000. This mortality rate is at least 20 percent higher than Europe's worst localized plague estimates of the Black Death in the fourteenth century.[8]

While B.C.'s First Nations did not experience the immediate loss of their primary food source, as did the Plains peoples, they did suffer many of the same things as First Nations bands further east. Like them, they were all eventually subject to the Indian Act in 1876. As with all First Nations, assimilation was the stated official policy of the B.C. and Canadian governments. However, just as on the Prairies, the contradictory, segregationist regulations within the Indian Act made assimilation an impossibility. First Nations were compelled to live on reserves, arbitrary restrictions were placed on their movement off reserve, and they were denied the vote. On the other hand, harsh measures were vigorously imposed to extinguish existing aboriginal culture. The Indian Act forbade their right to wear traditional clothing, and it outlawed specific traditional rituals and practices, such as potlach.

Potlatch was a centuries-old ritual of the Northwest First Nations and some interior tribes. It served as a time-tested means of redistributing wealth through gift giving, appointing band leaders, confirming in public any changes in status such as marriages, birth, death, and coming of age, and it also had a practical social purpose in the maintenance of relations between tribes. In 1884, the Indian Act banned the ceremony on the grounds that it was profligate, irresponsible, and reckless behaviour that undermined a band's economic vitality. Banning the ritual had far-reaching and negative social implications.

In addition to this, indigenous community leadership was further undermined as the Indian Act appointed Indian Agents who exercised administrative power on the reserve and became the band's sole official intermediary with the government. In yet another inconsistent measure that would prevent economic and social integration, Indian agents could and did arbitrarily choose to restrict the external sale of any agricultural produce or livestock raised by the band.

In British Columbia, attempts to destroy aboriginal culture were probably the result of high-handed, instinctive, and deeply ingrained assumptions of cultural superiority rather than the result of any specific attempt to clear the land for white settlement, as happened on the Prairies. Aboriginal settlements were generally remote, and by the time of the Confederation decades, aboriginal population densities were so low that they posed no threat or obstacle to migration and settlement.

At the outset of the Confederation period, the only settlement of any size in British Columbia was the tiny outpost of Victoria. Britain was keen to lay claim to Vancouver Island, and so established an isolated Hudson's Bay Company trading post on the island in 1843. Previously, the Hudson's Bay Company had run most of its operations from Fort Vancouver, which was then situated on the Columbia River in what is now Oregon.

West Coast First Nations attend a ceremony marking British Columbia's entry into Confederation.

As rich as British Columbia was in natural resources, it developed late as a colony. This was not for lack of interest, but because it was commercially accessible only by the long ocean routes around either the Cape of Good Hope or Cape Horn. The threat of American expansion westward once again aroused British and Canadian interest in securing the West coast as part of the British Empire.

Britain, sensing America's growing strength and aggressive temperament, was anxious to resolve by negotiation its ongoing boundary disputes with the United States. In June of 1846 the Oregon Treaty redefined the disputed boundaries between Oregon and New Caledonia, as the B.C. mainland was then known. The timing of the treaty was indicative of the new-found respect Britain had for an increasingly powerful United States. Just six weeks before the treaty's finalization, a bellicose America had declared war on Mexico. By the end of that war, America had added California, Utah, Nevada, Arizona, and New Mexico to its territory.

While British Columbia was by mid-century firmly and lawfully British, the only non-aboriginal settlements on the West Coast were the village of Victoria and a string of scattered fur trading posts. In 1858 that began to change as a result of the discovery of gold on the British Columbia mainland. Victoria and Vancouver Island went through a sudden metamorphosis. The village changed from being a trading post and insignificant maritime coaling station to being the capital of a colony in its own right, as well as the main commercial supply centre for gold miners headed to the gold fields on the Fraser River. Just as California had boomed between 1848 and 1855, Victoria and mainland British Columbia expanded at a feverish pace. Within the space of weeks, Victoria grew from three hundred people to over five thousand. Unable to control the flood of migrants to the lower mainland, Governor James Douglas recommended that the area be declared immediately open for settlement and the land sold for twenty shillings an acre.

The initial gold rush of 1858 petered out, but it was followed by another in the interior Cariboo region in 1860. This one created a boomtown of wooden huts, plank sidewalks, and shanties called Barkerville. It is estimated that in the early 1860s, Barkerville had a population of ten thousand people, making it the largest town in western Canada at that time. As in all gold rushes, the initial exhilaration and wild hopes were followed by hard reality.

Many eventually left Vancouver Island and the mainland, but that first spark of activity touched off a string of changes that would turn British Columbia into Canada's sixth province. Britain declared mainland British Columbia as a separate Crown colony in 1858. They were made one colony in 1866.

British Columbia joined Confederation in 1871. The conventional wisdom is that the delegates haggling over the terms of entry demanded that Canada had to build a railway connecting the Prairies to the Pacific coast. In fact, what the B.C. delegation asked for was far less dramatic. They simply wanted a wagon road. John A. Macdonald was the one who upped the ante and made the offer more attractive by proposing a railway instead.[9]

Like many of Macdonald's ideas, it was a shrewd move and a bold gamble. The Royal Engineers had built the Cariboo Road through the B.C. interior during the second gold rush. It was a tricky piece of engineering and was probably what focused the provincial delegates on the idea of building a second road. Macdonald likely realized that putting a railway through the mountains would take just as much work, and would have to be in place in any event if the province was to be commercially connected to the rest of the country on a year-round basis. The deal was made; Canada took on B.C.'s massive debt load and promised to link the coast with a transcontinental railway. But it was a much more difficult proposition than anyone anticipated. British Columbia didn't get its railway link to the coast for another fifteen years.

A wagon train in B.C.'s Cariboo Mountains, 1870s.

By the end of the Confederation decades, British Columbia's territory was half the size it is today. At the end of the 1870s, Vancouver was little more than a hamlet, with a sawmill, and a few shops, taverns, and houses perched around the Burrard Inlet. It was another six years before it was incorporated as a city. By 1880, the entire province was still not much more than an embryonic hinterland, and only had a population of less than fifty thousand people. That would all change once Macdonald's railway was completed, at which point the province began to industrialize and each decade averaged 70 percent population growth for the next forty years.

Inuit hunters cleaning a walrus after a hunt at the edge of the ice pack.

Canada's High North has been inhabited by the Inuit, a people who migrated out of what is now Alaska almost 1,200 years ago. The Inuit in turn were descendants of the Thule people who migrated from north-eastern Siberia over 4,000 years ago. As a cohesive aboriginal culture and people, the Inuit have the most extensive geographic range of all the world's traditional peoples, with communities stretching across Greenland, northern Canada, Alaska, and eastern Siberia.

Throughout the nineteenth century, they lived a traditional semi-nomadic lifestyle on a landscape that has changed very little since then: vast expanses of barren grounds and tundra populated with scattered herds of caribou and muskox as well as small populations of wolves, fox, arctic hare, and lemmings. The Arctic islands and coastal areas were home to seals and walrus packs as well as seventeen species of whales that migrated in the channels.

In winter and summer in the Canadian Arctic, the Inuit survived in extended family groups: hunting on the tundra in summer and fishing and sealing on frozen coastal areas in the winter. Their laws and traditions were passed down orally, and they followed a traditional animistic belief system of reverence for all things both living and inanimate.

Canada's High North saw the beginnings of change during the Confederation era. In the mid-nineteenth century there was intermittent contact between the Inuit and those of European descent. Most of the interactions between the two groups were between small, isolated Inuit communities and American whalers, hunting for narwhales, belugas, and oil-rich bowhead whales during the season's short, ice-free window. Periodically, there were a few encounters between explorers and Inuit. For the most part, all these contacts were amicable; and some, particularly those meetings with whalers, resulted in small-scale annual trading exchanges. Through these meetings, the Inuit were gradually introduced to firearms, cloth, metal, tools, cooking utensils, Western musical instruments, as well as alcohol and tobacco.

Although there was little overt conflict, the Inuit suffered terribly from these first encounters. Accurate statistics are difficult to come by, but the Inuit are believed to have suffered at least as much as the First Nations did from diseases introduced by Europeans. Some estimates place nineteenth-century Inuit deaths from disease as high as 90 percent.[10]

Their lifestyle was changed forever by the alien-looking men, who spoke bizarre sounding languages and arrived in strangely shaped ships. Perhaps the most famous of the alien-looking men of the Confederation era was Sir John Franklin, a Royal Navy officer, Trafalgar veteran, and an experienced, although obdurate, explorer. Franklin, who had been on three previous exploratory expeditions, was no stranger to the North. A previous overland expedition that he led to explore the Arctic coastline ended in near disaster. Franklin refused to listen to his aboriginal guides and trappers and mounted his expedition without making use of local sleighs or suitable clothing. Instead, his expedition wore British uniforms and brought with them mess china, silver, and table linens. Over the course of almost three years, he lost half of his men. The mission was plagued by mutiny, starvation, murder, and cannibalism. The expedition did have two redeeming outcomes: it furnished a good example of how not to run a northern expedition; and Franklin's maps and charts provided a much-improved appreciation of Canada's Arctic coastal areas.

Back in England, Franklin was hailed as a hero. In 1845, he was given command of two ships, the *Erebus* and the *Terror*, and tasked to find the Northwest Passage. The ships were provisioned for three years, and equipped with the latest scientific research instruments. Underestimating the distances involved, however, Franklin's vessels became trapped in the ice near King William Island. The crews struck out on foot and tried to make their way overland to safety, when they realized their ships would likely be crushed in the shifting ice.

Uncovering the fate of the Franklin expedition became a *cause célèbre* in Victorian society. A total of twenty-six missions were sent out in search of the lost Franklin Expedition, but little was heard of them — except for a three-man gravesite and Inuit reports of an abandoned ice-bound ship and starving sailors trying to seek safety. A further three graves were discovered on Beechey Island in the 1980s. Thirty-four years later, Canadian Coast Guard divers found the wreck of the *Erebus* lying upright in eleven metres of water on the sea bed of Queen Maud Gulf. The *Terror* was discovered two years later in 2016, well to the south, submerged, but in good condition.

Franklin's voyage was certainly the most famous of the Arctic expeditions during the Confederation era, but it was far from being the only one. There were many other exploratory missions to Canada's North launched by British, American, Austro-Hungarian, Dutch, German, and Norwegian explorers, but, significantly, no Canadians tried to explore the region. Nonetheless, despite its lack of presence in the Arctic, Canada extended its claims of sovereignty over its current Arctic borders in 1880.

Chapter Eight

THE IMMIGRANT PEOPLES:
THE IRISH

By contemporary standards, mid-nineteenth-century Canada was a remarkably homogenous society. While today, most people who trace their heritage back to the United Kingdom would likely refer to their ancestry as British, the very first set of census takers scrupulously recorded anglophone national origins as being English, Scottish, and Irish.* As we've seen, these earliest census takers muddied the demographic waters by refusing to acknowledge that "American" was a distinct culture. They recorded the growing number of American settlers by referencing their more distant national origins. When Canada's first national census was undertaken in 1871, the process had evolved considerably and this deficiency was fixed.

The 1871 census provided a thorough reckoning of the new country. It asked 211 questions ranging over a wide variety of topics. The four provinces were subdivided into 1,701 sub-districts, and information was collected on 3,485,761 people. We now have a statistical understanding of much of the minutiae of national life: how many horned cattle the country had, how many yards of homemade linen were spun, and how many barrels of medicinal cod liver oil were produced. A staff of under fifty people collated the final report, and two years later produced a bilingual, hard-bound, three-volume record of the nation's statistics. In 1879, Parliament tasked the Census Bureau to increase the scope of its efforts, to include any territories that might be added, as well as to conduct "collection, abstraction, tabulation and publication of vital agricultural, commercial, criminal and other statistics."[1]

---

* The Welsh, being a small and presumably affable minority, were often lumped in statistically with the English.

Immigration to Canada from 1760 until 1812 was mostly from the United States. During and after the American Revolutionary War, United Empire Loyalists came to Canada in their tens of thousands. At the time, it was very dangerous to remain loyal to Britain in many parts of America. Loyalty to the Crown was frequently viewed as treason, and confiscation of one's land, vigilante justice, and the practice of smearing "Tories" with boiling tar and feathers was not uncommon. However, contrary to popular notions, not all Loyalists were of British background, and not all came to Canada because they had an abiding and fervent loyalty to the British Crown. Some were seeking religious freedom, some were First Nations who had allied themselves with Britain, some were recent black slaves promised their freedom, and some came for the promise of free land. Nevertheless, they were all gratefully accepted by colonial governments anxious to develop their territories.

The welcome reception of American immigrants ended promptly with the War of 1812. With the outbreak of war, American settlers were viewed with suspicion, and immigration from Britain quickly replaced the settlers streaming into Canada from the United States.

Although there was Loyalist emigration to the Atlantic provinces, British settlement had been well-established there for many years. Four years before creating the Red River settlement, in P.E.I., Lord Selkirk established his first immigrant farming communities of Highland Scots who had been evicted from their small acreages to make room for sheep in the clearances. Shortly after, waves of Irish immigrants followed.

Prior to the Confederation era, Canada had seen relatively small-scale and sporadic Irish immigration. The Irish had been amongst the very first to settle in Atlantic Canada. Newfoundland had the first recorded Irish settlements as early 1675. In the 1830s, several hundred Irish settlers homesteaded in coastal villages in the Maritimes, but later in the decade many moved to more fertile areas in the interior river valleys. Most of the Irish in these initial waves were Protestants from Ulster who were escaping the rising cost of land, crowded rural conditions, and declining employment opportunities. By the end of the 1830s, a large proportion of these Irish immigrants migrated to cities and towns — almost certainly because they did not want to go back to farming after their harsh and unprofitable experiences as farmers back in Ireland. As a result, by the mid-1840s, cities like Halifax had large Irish populations. By comparison with later waves of Irish immigration, these initial arrivals were reasonably prosperous. Things were soon to change drastically. By 1845, Ireland was to experience the first of six seasons of a devastating potato blight, massive starvation, and a tidal wave of migration that saw the country's population plunge by almost 25 percent.

The Great Famine in Ireland was the result of a nationwide potato blight. The crop failure was caused by a mold that attacked the leaves and edible roots of the potato plant. It was a catastrophe that grew into a disaster of biblical proportions. For over a hundred years, Irish farmers had raised only two different strains of potatoes. They were simple to grow, nourishing, and could regularly produce yields capable of feeding a large family on Ireland's tiny farm plots, most of which were less than six acres. Shortly after the potato's introduction to Ireland, it became the nation's most important crop, with more than half the country depending exclusively on potatoes as a dietary staple. The crop failed for six consecutive years.

Within weeks of the potato blight's first appearance, crops across the country began to wilt and rot in the fields. No one was prepared for such a disaster. Ireland had few reserves of food, and famine quickly set in. Instead of relief, the government in London initially established hard-labour, public works projects, and imported limited amounts of corn from North America. These programs were abandoned as too costly in 1847, and three million Irish, almost all of them Catholic peasant farmers, became dependent on an entirely inadequate program of soup kitchens funded by the government in London. By the autumn of 1847, people were dying in droves from starvation. The soup kitchen program was then closed and replaced with a program set up under locally administered "Poor Laws."

The program of Poor Laws was established to remove the burden of providing for famine relief from the government in London. The new scheme transferred responsibility for feeding the starving Irish population to local landowners. Under these new laws, to be eligible for relief, hungry Irish families had to abandon their farms and live in squalid workhouses. There were not enough workhouses to meet the demand, however, and many of those that were opened had to close for lack of funding. In addition to the famine, related diseases took a huge toll.

Dysentery, cholera, smallpox, influenza, typhoid, and what was generically called "fever" killed thousands.

Despite the utter destitution in Ireland, wealthy absentee Irish landlords were shipping surplus produce to mainland Britain, and Britain was, in turn, exporting food to mainland Europe. The British public knew of the catastrophe taking place fifty miles across the Irish Sea, yet there was remarkably little sympathy or outcry anywhere in Britain for their plight. The government, professing an unshakeable belief in free trade, refused to spend money on the problem, as the very thought of public charity ran contrary to its absolutist views on placing undue restraints on either government or commerce.

The acting treasury minister, Sir Charles Trevelyan, who was responsible for handling the Irish famine, proclaimed that the "problem of Irish overpopulation being altogether beyond the power of man, the cure had been supplied by the direct stroke of an all-wise Providence."[2] Under his watch, a million men, women, and children starved to death, and almost two million people emigrated to England, the United States, Canada, and Australia. Trevelyan was knighted in 1848 for his services to government.

Those who were lucky enough to escape to Canada faced several appalling sets of difficulties. The landowners, unwilling to spend money on poor houses, instead chose the least expensive route and simply evicted the farmers for failure to pay their rent, or, in many cases, paid the fares to ship starving peasant families to Canada. More often than not, desperate Irish farmers would be told that upon arrival in Canada they would be welcomed as valued immigrants and provided an allowance as well as shelter, food, and clothing. It was a cruel fraud. Distressed and starving, they believed the tale. The landowners were confident in knowing that should their former tenants survive the three-thousand-mile ocean voyage, they would have no means of ever returning to make a claim against them.

By early June 1847, fourteen thousand Irish immigrants arrived in Quebec. It was the largest and easily the most dramatic migration ever to reach Canada. They were the first of the famine migrants and were crammed into the holds of forty hastily converted timber ships. The ships rode at anchor in a two-mile line down the St. Lawrence, thirty miles downstream from Quebec City, all waiting to disembark their passengers at Grosse Isle for a medical inspection.

Thousands of Irish migrated to Canada in unmodified "coffin ships" like these.

In getting to Grosse Isle, the surviving passengers endured a horrific journey. The average sea voyage took two to three months, with families stuffed together in dank, dark, rolling, unheated timber holds with no semblance of comfort or privacy. Food and fresh water were revolting and inadequate. Toilets were wooden buckets. Two Canadian priests, who visited one "coffin ship" after it docked, described walking in holds that left them up to their ankles in human filth. There was no means of keeping clean and medical facilities or assistance was non-existent. No one was enforcing the existing regulations, so even the crudest standards of hygiene and safety were ignored. As a result, the mortality rate on the voyage, depending on the ship, was between 30 and 40 percent.

The voyage of the *Virginius* from Liverpool was not unusual for the ships making that journey during those early years of the famine. After leaving Ireland in 1847 with 476 passengers on board, 158 (including 9 crew members) died in transit. Arriving at Grosse Isle, a further 106 were diagnosed with fever. People died most frequently of typhus, but dysentery and cholera were also widespread. For the next five years, lines of ships, all with similar tales and comparable statistics, would queue up off Grosse Isle, waiting to disembark their passengers at Canada's entry point quarantine station.

Once ashore at Grosse Isle, immigrants would almost always find the primitive medical facilities overwhelmed. The survivors of the ocean voyage were invariably sick and weakened. Five thousand Irish are buried on the island.

The few temporary wooden sheds at Grosse Isle were quickly filled to overflowing with the people from the first ship. For the next several months, the island's staff tried to house sick refugees on the dirt floors of tents, but as the tents soon filled, people were stretched out on the open ground. Meals were worse than aboard the coffin ships: tea, porridge, or a weak broth served three times a day. New sheds were eventually built, but in insufficient numbers, with no proper beds and no ventilation or toilet facilities. The sick were bedded down regardless of sex or age, with two people head to foot on boards. Exhausted nursing staff, whose numbers were greatly reduced by contracted illness, were at one point relieved by prisoners who had been pressed into service. The convicts were worse than useless; they stole the personal effects of the dying.

However, it was by no means all sordid. There was conspicuous heroism. Nurses, doctors, orderlies, clergy, and volunteers often worked themselves to the point of collapse, dozens of them, including the mayor of Montreal, dying beside their patients.[3]

When refugee numbers became too great, harried doctors, many often mortally sick themselves, did the most cursory of inspections onboard ship. Striding past lines of bedraggled men, women, and children, they would direct that those who showed no obvious signs of fever be allowed to carry on to Montreal or points west.[4]

From Grosse Isle, the refugees were sent on, usually by barge, to Montreal. Thousands, carrying latent infections, would fall ill within two weeks. Near what is now the neighborhood of Pointe-Saint-Charles in Montreal, several thousand more refugees died of typhus in the fever sheds. Nobody is certain of the exact numbers. With orphaned children and illiterate, undocumented adults dying in their scores each day, record keeping was not a priority. The dead were hastily buried with little ceremony in mass graves. The area in Pointe-Saint-Charles was cordoned off by the militia to prevent unauthorized access, or the escape of infected patients. Many of the refugees who showed no symptoms in Montreal were crammed onto open barges, shivering in their rags at night, blistered by the sun and soaked by the rains as they slowly made their way further upstream to Kingston and Toronto. For thousands more, the same fate awaited them in hastily built fever sheds along the shores of Lake Ontario.

Of those who survived the ordeal of their voyage, more than half moved on to the United States as soon as they possibly could. Anxious to leave behind any ties to the British Crown, and urged on by reports of easy employment and security, many of these migrants found themselves discriminated against and marginalized by a hostile Protestant culture.

Things were no better in Canada. Many Irish Protestants who had emigrated years earlier were deeply antagonistic to their fellow countrymen, and the arrival of large numbers of Irish Catholics gave a huge boost to the formation of Orange Lodges across English Canada.[5] In the English community, the feelings of cultural superiority and racial animosity so prevalent back in Britain, were displayed in an only slightly muted version in Canada. It was not uncommon to see signs in shop windows and newspapers that read, *Help Wanted — No Irish Need Apply*.

The Irish, like so many immigrant groups, tended to settle near others from similar backgrounds. Large

A typical Irish working man, Ontario, 1860s.

Irish Catholic communities rapidly sprang up in Montreal, Quebec City, Kingston, Toronto, and dozens of smaller villages and towns. A sizeable percentage of Irish Catholics, for the same reasons as their fellow Protestant countrymen, preferred to settle in urban areas. For many, bitter memories of hard-scrabble farming and hunger were all too vivid. With little education and few marketable skills, they found employment as labourers in the mills and in the timber and construction trades.

Those who chose to, and those with no other alternatives, went back to farming, some working initially as hired hands while some, thoroughly hardened by their background, chose to carve out their future as homesteaders.

Like so many of Canada's resilient immigrant groups, the Irish have had a hugely positive influence on Canada. Theirs was not an easy path. They had to overcome the period's vicious caricatures of them as violent, disloyal, prone to drunkenness, and indolent. But over the course of a few decades, as religious tolerance grew and the Irish repeatedly proved their worth, the bigotry, exclusion, and marginalization decreased, and they took their rightful place as a vigorous and essential part of the Canadian mosaic.

Chapter Nine

THE IMMIGRANT PEOPLES: THE SCOTS

The third-largest ethnic group in Canada are the decedents of the Scots, who have, for several centuries, been one of the most influential ethnicities in Canada. Although that's certainly an accolade that they share with several other groups of people, it is undeniable that the Scots have been instrumental in giving Canada much of its character.

The first Scottish settlers in Canada came as early as 1622, when Sir William Alexander brought Scottish settlers to the Maritimes to establish a New Scotland for King James. Sir William must have been a classically educated man, as the new colony was grandiosely dubbed "Nova Scotia." The province has maintained its unique Scottish disposition for almost four centuries and the Scots have been prominent in virtually every aspect of the country's development since then.

During the Confederation decades, the Scots played an enormous role in molding the nation's institutions, culture, and personality. Scots have provided the majority of Canada's prime ministers; they were amongst our earliest anglophone settlers; they ran the two great fur trading companies; they have made an indelible mark on our armed forces; created many of our most prestigious universities; and been disproportionately represented in business, medicine, the arts, law, science, and engineering.[1] However, that being the case, it begs the question of why the Scots should have wielded such influence?

The answer surely lies in the eighteenth century, a hundred years before the Confederation decades, and before the first substantial waves of Scottish migration reached Canada. Modern Scottish character has been in large measure influenced by the Scottish Enlightenment, a movement that is directly reflected in many institutions and traditions of modern Canada.

The Scottish Enlightenment had its beginnings in Scotland's universities. Scotland's ancient university traditions date back to the late Middle Ages, and, as a result, the Scots have always had a unique focus and reverence for learning and knowledge. In the mid-eighteenth century, a new spirit of free inquiry took root in virtually all fields of study in Scotland. In a spirit of uninhibited analysis, Scottish academics addressed issues ranging from philosophy, economics, geology, art, medicine, architecture, law, economics, archeology, and engineering. The catalyst for this new approach was the beginning of an era of specialization in Scottish academic life, where instead of having one teacher lead a student through his entire curriculum, the universities evolved to have individuals who were highly specialized in one given field. The concept of having a dedicated professor researching and teaching a single subject was, in its day, revolutionary, and it spurred a new way of thinking. Scotland was a small territory and the new approach to free enquiry spread rapidly beyond the walls of the universities. Lawyers, doctors, clergymen, writers, and artists became imbued with this new mindset. In addition to a revolution within the universities, Scotland became obsessive about ensuring its children were educated. By the mid-eighteenth century, it had twice as many universities as England and the highest rates of literacy in the world. By the turn of the century, the city of Edinburgh alone had sixteen publishing houses. As a culture, the Scots prized knowledge, inquiry, and learning; and primary and secondary education, while not always accessible to many, was highly regarded. Scotland produced men like David Hume, who wrote daring new books, such as *A Treatise of Human Nature*, on a systematic and scientific way of thinking about the study of human nature; Adam Smith, the Scottish father of political economy, wrote *The Wealth of Nations*, a book that inspired the rise of modern economic theory and democratic capitalism; and James Watt, a Scottish polymath who was greatly influenced by the spirit of the times, was an inventor, engineer, and entrepreneur who revolutionized the steam engine.

The thinkers of the early period of the Scottish enlightenment were followed by generations of Scots who shared and expanded their rationalist and humanist approach to learning and inquiry. They believed that mankind, following the principles of reason and practical empirical inquiry, could always do much better. It became a part of the Scottish tradition that was exported to the Scottish diaspora. It's a tradition that still exists today in schools, governments, architecture, the sciences, and business.[2]

However, it would be wrong to portray Scotland as an intellectual Garden of Eden. It had its darker side. Despite the Scottish Enlightenment, the highlands were populated by impoverished subsistence farmers and crofters living on rented farms. During the Confederation decades, half of all the land in Scotland was owned by sixty-eight families.[3] The image of the highland crofter has undergone a romanticized image makeover since the Confederation era. The image of the sturdy independent highland farmer or aristocrat in his bonnet and kilt was largely a dreamy Victorian invention, popularized by Queen Victoria's obsession with things Scottish. Crofters were poor farmers who lived hand-to-mouth on a year-to-year basis on "crofts" — tiny leased farms with small gardens and pasturage usually for a handful of cattle. Crofter families supplemented their incomes picking kelp from the sea shores to sell for use in manufacturing potash and iodine. Seasonal fishing and voluntary enlistment in the highland regiments of the British Army also became not only iconic professions for the Scots, but also significant sources of income for impoverished families.

With the repeal of the Corn Laws and its newfound fervency for self-regulating economies and free trade came the second round of Scottish land clearances. Much as it happened in the eighteenth century, many of the remaining crofters were forcibly moved off their lands so that their farms could be used for the more profitable practice of turning them into sheep and large-scale cattle pasturage. The crofters had few legal protections, and their evictions ordered by absentee landlords were sudden and often violent. In the early phases of the nineteenth-century clearances, many crofters were, without notice, dragged from their homes and had their cottages burned behind them. To make matters worse, in the late 1840s, the potato blight that had such a catastrophic effect on Ireland had spread to Scotland. Its effect was not as dramatic as in Ireland, because Scottish diets were more varied, but it caused serious inflation, hardship, and real hunger. The early Confederation decades were grim times in Scotland and displaced Scots desperately searching for work streamed into the newly crowded lowland cities of Glasgow, Edinburgh, and northern England. They also migrated to Canada in their thousands.

Confederation-era Scots most frequently moved to Ontario, which was a change from earlier decades when they tended to settle in the Maritimes. Most of the newcomers were Presbyterian, and most spoke English, although there was a sizeable percentage of Roman Catholics and Gaelic speakers. The religious animosity between Protestant and Catholic Scots was not nearly as pronounced or as virulent as it was amongst the Irish, but there was very little intermarriage, as it was actively discouraged, and when choosing a settlement, the two groups invariably gravitated to their own communities. In the early years of the Confederation decades, Gaelic was the third most common European language spoken in Canada.

The crush of Scottish immigrants lasted long after the clearances. By the 1860s, immigrants were streaming into Canada from a cross-section of the Scottish population. Many who came were farmers searching for lands of their own, but there were also artisans of every description: blacksmiths, carpenters, millwrights, metal workers, and carriage makers are listed in the immigrant rolls, as were large numbers of professionals seeking a new life and new opportunities. Most notable among the professionals were significant numbers of teachers, clergy, and engineers. All of them would exert a defining influence in Ontario and the newly settled West.

Several writers in the past two decades have developed the notion that the Scots and the Irish have been one of the key influences in determining the character of the modern world.[4] There is unquestionably a degree of truth to this, but it is probably not inclusive enough an explanation of the larger reality lurking deep in our national psyche. Without parsing the DNA

Talented artisans from Scotland brought valuable skills to Confederation-era Canada. This prosperous blacksmith shop in Ontario was a typical small business of the period.

of the problem, it's probable that the Celtic influence in Canada is even broader and deeper than originally assumed. After all, the French in Canada are largely descended from Normans and Bretons, who in their distant past were also Celtic peoples. So, it is very likely that much of Canada's early personality was at least in part a happy, coincidental meeting of, if not always like-minded people, certainly similarly synthesized ones. For the Scots, the French, and the Irish have exhibited the highest degree of national co-operation and this combination of sensibilities has done much to define Canada's future.

While cobbling together racial theories to explain history can often be foolish and dangerous, it's fair and reasonable to suggest that the four European cultures that had such an impact on the Confederation decades shared some deep-rooted cultural resemblances — all of which have over the course of time been greatly influenced by the Scottish Enlightenment. The prime features of the Scottish Enlightenment — pragmatic rationalism, a courageous sense of inquiry, a continual quest for improvement, and a belief in humanism — have without question been driving factors in developing our present notions of accepting diversity in our society. We have much to be grateful for to those Confederation-era Scots who helped lay the foundations to make Canadians accepting of a richer and diverse infusion of cultures and experiences — and that characteristic has today become the defining feature of our national personality.

Chapter Ten

THE IMMIGRANT PEOPLES:
THE FRENCH

In the decades following the Quebec uprising of 1837–38, the province's social and economic order began a steady but gradual transformation. This was due to several developments. Quebec's rural society underwent a mild but prolonged crisis, one that had its origins in unsupportable population growth, outdated agricultural practices, and the social disruption that invariably accompanies demographic and technological changes.

The spectacular growth in the rural population between 1759 and 1840 imposed economic and social pressures on the old seigneurially based society. Not surprisingly, the province's farms and villages had been unable to support the rapid population increase. Many of those who weren't going to inherit their family farm moved into the cities, or joined the tens of thousands of francophone Quebecers who migrated to work for higher wages in New England's factories.

Making things worse, arable land had also become scarce in the province. The soils on existing farms were showing signs of depletion, and crop yields were slowly declining. To further complicate things, farming methods had not kept up with modern practices and agricultural technologies were behind the times.

On the other hand, positive change did come about with the abolition of the seigneurial system in 1854. Farmers now had title to their own land. This was an enormous change in Quebec's society, but it did not show immediate results. The economic effects of this development would take years to register, as the province's farmers slowly but steadily accrued capital.

Other aspects of the economy were in a similar state of flux. The fur trade was in gradual but steady decline. The timber trade, however, was growing, and this meant that many French-speaking Quebecers found secure employment in the province's booming forest industry.

Rural French Quebec was not alone in facing the kind of upheaval that went along with industrialization. Similar issues were ongoing, or had taken place, in most European countries. In their analyses of social change in Quebec during this period, some historians have been defensive about the turmoil experienced in the province; however, in retrospect, we can see that these symptoms are normal indicators of the dramatic changes imposed on a society as it shifts from an agrarian to an industrial economy. What was extraordinary about Quebec was that the province's evolution from a rural to a modern urban society was tranquil, gradual, and far less traumatic than that of the Irish or Scots immigrants who came to the country during the Confederation era — and certainly much more peaceful than most European nations. Quebecers faced nothing

Merchants' houses, Pointe-Lévis, Quebec, early 1870s.

like the trauma that confronted Britain, France, Italy, or Germany during their periods of industrialization. As a rural, self-contained society, Quebec was lucky. The province was well-insulated from much of the painful social turmoil that marked the onset of the Industrial Revolution elsewhere. It was comfortably self-sufficient, while it remained politically and economically stable.

This is not to say that Quebec's French-speaking population was a society without tensions. The rise of a small middle class, centred primarily in Quebec City and Montreal, prompted the growth of a peaceful but spirited conflict between the Church and the new bourgeoisie. The new French-speaking middle class was a small one and arose mainly from the province's liberal professions: notaries, doctors, and lawyers, as well as a small but growing class of successful urban merchants. From this new middle class emerged liberal ideas and attitudes that challenged the old system.

The Parti Rouge became the political embodiment of this new kind of thinking. As a social movement, the Parti Rouge had its distant origins in the wake of the rebellions of 1837-38, and in a uniquely Quebecois institution, the Institut canadien in Montreal. Because Montreal did not have a university at the time, a group of the city's new middle class established the Institut in 1844. The Institut was founded to serve the city as a kind of literary and debating salon as well as a scientific association. Its members were free thinkers, and most were deeply worried that, with the union of Upper and Lower Canada, their French identity and future would be swamped; as such, they were strongly opposed to the new political order.

Les Rouges had several other issues on their agenda. They were the political spur for the abolition of the seigneurial system; they demanded universal suffrage; and they agitated for the province to have its own elected legislative council, judges, and governor general. Many of the Parti Rouge's members wanted immediate commercial reciprocity with the United States, while some advocated outright for the province's annexation by the United States. Most tellingly, they promoted secular education and were vigorous advocates of the separation of church and state.

All these views naturally brought them into opposition with the Tories and other conservative elements in society, but their fiercest opponents were in the Roman Catholic Church.

During the Confederation era in Quebec, the Catholic Church's role and importance grew considerably. It is impossible to say what precisely caused this, but the ideas emanating from the Institut canadien and the formation of Les Rouges as a political force certainly acted as stimuli to the Church taking a more active role in the province's political life.

However, Catholic influence in Quebec was not just political. There was a profound deepening of religious conviction in Quebec during the Confederation era. Between 1840 and 1896, church attendance for francophones in Quebec increased dramatically, from 40 to 98 percent. With religious observance skyrocketing, the Catholic Church also saw an enormous growth in the number of clergy and an unprecedented rise in the number of religious orders and institutions established in Quebec. During the Confederation era, eighteen new major congregations of brothers and nuns sprang up in the province, and the total number of priests in Quebec grew by 800 percent.[1]

During these years, a religious school of thought called "ultramontanism" gained acceptance within much of Quebec's Catholic clergy. Ultramontanism had its beginnings in Europe, and was largely a response to the Church's diminished influence following the wave of secular revolutionary fervour that swept France during the French Revolution. The central tenets of ultramontanism were the supremacy of religious authority over civil society and the doctrine of papal infallibility in matters of faith and morals. Ultramontanism didn't begin to take hold in Quebec until some three-and-a-half decades after its appearance in Europe, but when it did, conflict between the new generation of free thinkers in the Institut and the Catholic Church was inevitable.

The Church was bitterly opposed to virtually all the ideas coming from the Institut canadien. For its part, the Church in mid-nineteenth-century Quebec saw the existing political system as entirely satisfactory. It left the Church in the key role it had played since 1759. It was not only society's paramount moral authority, it was the champion for French-language rights and French culture, and it maintained the system of confessional Catholic schools. The Institut canadien posed a deadly threat to this system. Its members openly challenged the Church's assumption that it was the overseer and watchdog of the province's moral standards and not one's individual conscience. Eventually, after years of bitter public argument, the Bishop of Montreal decreed that, under pain of excommunication, no Catholic could belong to the Institut while it taught "pernicious doctrines" and its library circulated banned books that were anti-clerical in nature. The Bishop of Montreal was eventually forced by the Vatican to retire for his involvement in secular politics, but the threat of excommunication was a body blow to "radical" thinking in the province. Over the years, the Institut's membership and activities steadily decreased, and the Institut finally closed its doors in 1880. Les Rouges eventually softened their political doctrines, and, adopting a more practical compromise with the rest of Canada, they in turn joined the "Clear Grits" to form the Liberal Party of Canada.

While the Church in Quebec during the Confederation era was well-known for its forays into politics, it generally gets much less credit than it deserves for its important social work during the time. The Church in Quebec was heavily committed to, and invested in, education, health care, and charitable work. Unlike in Britain or in America's newly industrialized cities, Quebec's cities avoided many of the cruelest aspects of Victorian life. Life in those cities was certainly no paradise, but Quebec's social evolution was much less harsh and exhibited fewer of the kinds of evils Charles Dickens described during the era. The poor got some elementary schooling; orphans were not left to roam the streets; the problems of the corruption and exploitation of children were not as great; and the province had fewer class issues and conflicts between those with newly acquired wealth and the growing urban proletariat. The Catholic Church essentially provided virtually all of Quebec's social services. Schools, hospitals, homes for the destitute, asylums, orphanages, and almost all public charities were run by the Church — contributing substantially to the betterment of Quebec society at virtually no cost to the government.

Canada's second largest French-speaking community, the Acadians, experienced a demographic resurgence during the Confederation era. With families frequently having a dozen or more children, the Acadian population jumped with each generation, growing from 8,500 at the turn of the century to over 140,000 by 1900.[2]

Acadian history in the Maritimes had until the nineteenth century been tragic. In 1713, the Acadians became British subjects after the Treaty of Utrecht ended the War of the Spanish Succession and the Acadian colony in Nova Scotia was ceded to the British. For forty-two years they lived peaceably as reluctant British subjects, but in 1755 they were forcibly expelled from their homes in Nova Scotia, Prince Edward Island, and New Brunswick.

The expulsion order was given by Charles Lawrence, the British governor in Halifax during the Seven Years' War. The war in the Maritimes had largely been a desultory conflict, consisting of a series of small-scale raids and alternating attempts by the French and English to seize one another's forts. After the British discovered nearly three hundred Acadian militiamen defending Fort Beauséjour in New Brunswick, Lawrence ordered Nova Scotia's French population to be forcibly deported and their lands and goods seized. There was no credible strategic rationale behind the expulsion, as the Acadian farmers posed no military threat. However, Lawrence ordered the expulsion when the Acadians refused to take an oath of loyalty to the British.

The more plausible motive behind the mass deportation was that envious English-speaking colonists from the Boston area influenced Lawrence. A vocal group of New England colonists had long argued that the Acadians were an "alien" people living in British lands, and for several years they lobbied to take over the Acadians' cleared and fertile farmlands. The militia volunteers and the loaded wording of the proposed oath gave them the excuse they had been seeking. Approximately ten thousand Acadians were deported, and several thousand others escaped to Quebec or hid in the woods. As soon as the Acadians moved out of Nova Scotia, settlers from New England began to move in.

In 1764 the expulsion order was lifted, and from that point right up until 1820 a stream of Acadians returned to the Maritimes. This time, they settled in Cape Breton, P.E.I., and northeastern New Brunswick.

The nineteenth-century Acadian resurgence has been called the "Acadian Renaissance." Not only did the Acadian population soar during the Confederation era, but in this period they rediscovered an enduring sense of pride and identity and began to actively assert their political will.

Initially, after their return to the Maritimes, Acadians were distrustful of their neighbours and did their best to shun most kinds of contact with their fellow anglophone citizens. In the first six decades after the return, Acadian communities were relatively isolated, self-reliant, economically withdrawn, and inwardly focused, surviving largely on a subsistence basis. By the Confederation era, that began to change.

The Maritime provinces were self-governing colonies, and, by excluding themselves from the political process, the Acadians realized that, despite their increasing numbers, their interests and voices were not being heard. More alarmingly, their leaders realized that in a changing world, unless they changed and changed quickly, they would soon be assimilated. Local leaders in the three provinces stood for election to the colonial legislatures and quickly became a force to be reckoned with — and in doing so further fanned nationalist feeling.

Somewhat like in Quebec, but less obtrusively in the Maritimes, the Catholic Church played a key role in nurturing pride and leading the Acadian nationalist movement. In 1864, the Collège Saint-Joseph, (the forerunner of the University of Moncton) was founded as an Acadian post-secondary institution. The Collège was to become a key factor in molding leaders and moving

A kelp wagon on an Acadian farm, Nova Scotia, 1870s.

the Acadian cause forward. In 1880, after attending a St. Jean Baptiste conference in Quebec City, the Acadian delegates came home inspired by Quebecois pride, but also more than ever determined not to be assimilated into Quebec's larger French-Canadian culture. In subsequent conferences of their own, Acadians approved the adoption of their own national anthem and a flag based on France's tricolor with the addition of a gold Papal star. That tradition of holding conferences and congresses to advance common Acadian issues continues to this day.

Since reasserting their national pride and unique culture during the Confederation decades, Acadians have never looked back. Far from being assimilated, by building upon traditions of self-respect, forebearance, and hard work, their culture and institutions have flourished. In preserving their way of life and heritage, they have been a peaceful example to the world of what can be accomplished through dignity and patience.

Chapter Eleven

THE IMMIGRANT PEOPLES:
THE ENGLISH

Canadians of English ancestry form the largest ethnic community in the country but, curiously, they are also the least visible of all the traditional groups.

Unlike the French, Irish, Scots, and Canada's many other immigrant groups, the English don't celebrate a particular holiday of their own — they have no day like St. Jean Baptiste Day, St. Patrick's Day, or Robbie Burns Night. They have almost no festivals or reunions; they rarely celebrate historical dates or anniversaries; yet their presence is everywhere. It is not that English Canadians have been taken for granted or ignored; instead, like familiar wallpaper, they have become so ordinary that they are virtually unnoticed.

The most likely reason for this is that Canadians of English descent have never had to fit in. They have always been, if not the dominant culture, one of the most influential. English laws, institutions, language, and culture permeate almost every aspect of Canadian society. Canadians of all backgrounds have knowingly or unconsciously adopted and internalized English symbols and traditions and made them their own. Nobody thinks it strange that Canadian parliamentary democracy and all its rituals reflect an English custom, that the army's most famous French-Canadian regiment mounts the guard on Quebec's citadel dressed in bearskins and scarlet tunics, that Canadian laws date back to the Magna Carta, or that hundreds of other traditions we see as being a part of Canada are copied from England. English influence has been accepted in Canada for the same reason it has been accepted in places like India. English culture is amenable to local mutation. English customs in Canada are a hybrid relation of those of the parent country. The cultural DNA has similarities, but it has traced its own unique evolutionary path. In Canada, adopting English culture has never been the nation's default mode; but those English traditions that we do have are widely accepted and now exhibit their own uniquely Canadian characteristics.

The people who brought those traditions to Canada migrated here in a number of distinct waves. Paradoxically, the first large-scale "English" migration to Canada was not from England, but from the United States. Following the American Revolution, the United Empire Loyalists moved north and settled in New Brunswick, Prince Edward Island, Ontario, and Quebec's Eastern Townships. Americans have never been given their due credit for this because, over the course of several early censuses, American immigrants tended to be lumped in with the English. Although no official reason has ever been forwarded for this bizarre accounting inaccuracy, it was probably a result of two things: deliberate misrepresentation, reflecting the unfortunate but traditional tendency to downgrade American influence in Canada; and, in the early days of settlement, a tendency by American loyalists and follow-on settlers, anxious to display their loyalty to the Crown, to claim English heritage rather than their more recent American lineage.

With the offer of free land, American settlers also moved up into southern Ontario in significant numbers prior to the War of 1812. This ceased abruptly once hostilities started and, for the next three decades thereafter, "English" immigration came largely from Britain, in what has been called the "Great Migration" — large numbers of immigrants from across England came to Canada, settling predominantly in the Maritimes. But by 1830, this pattern had changed. For several years, settlers came almost entirely from Yorkshire and moved to Canada West.

During those early years, the Canada Company, a commercial enterprise that saw the possibility of profit in the immigration and early land development business, brought in English immigrants to what is now western Ontario. These early settlers enjoyed mixed results. Many of the immigrants the Canada Company tried to settle in the first years of the Great Migration were poor farm hands who had experienced crop failures back home. A large percentage were unemployable, and many had been languishing in parish workhouses. As a result, many of the company's clients did not have the farming skills or the inclination to make a go of it, and did not stay in Canada, but instead moved on to settle in the United States. However, in the years just prior to Confederation, this exodus was offset by increased American immigration to Canada. Throughout the mid-and late nineteenth century, this would become a fairly consistent pattern, with Canadians and Americans migrating north and south. Canadians were invariably looking for jobs in the newly industrializing northern states, and Americans were searching for free land on which to carve out a homestead and farm.

By 1851 there were around 93,000 people in Ontario who had actually been born in England. These recent immigrants were by no means the majority. There were almost an equal number of Scots; and the Irish, who had begun emigrating to Canada in ever larger numbers, registered almost two and a half times as many new arrivals as the English. During the later Confederation decades, Irish immigration began to tail off and English immigration once again picked up, so that by 1871, 22 percent of Canada's entire population had been born in England.

The English who moved to Canada from the late 1850s onward came from varied backgrounds. Some were poor, but unlike many in the Irish and the early Scottish migrations, most English settlers could afford the price of a ticket. They were less desperate and more assured of finding employment or a successful niche in Canada. English arrivals often had skilled trades and had little difficulty becoming established. There were, however, other groups of English settlers who did not fit this mold.

Perhaps the most singular group in this category were "remittance men." From the late 1870s through the First World War, when this practice ceased, a surprising number of sons of the wealthy English upper classes, who for one reason or another were deemed troublesome or an embarrassment to their families, were packed off to Canada with an allowance — often not an overly generous one. They were expected never to return.

A few lived a life of indolence and leisure, joining some of the exclusive men's clubs in Montreal or Toronto, but most others ended up trying their hands at more demanding undertakings, such as commercial logging, homesteading, and ranching. As the Canadian West was settled, these men became the butt of popular jokes and music hall sketches.

In all likelihood, many of these young men experienced great difficulties adapting. Shunned at home and ridiculed in the new country, life was undoubtedly difficult. Many, by virtue of their background and disposition, were temperamentally unsuited for the rigors of a harsh, outdoor frontier life, while others quietly made a success of themselves.

Another large group of immigrants were the "home children." They were orphaned and abandoned children who had been given free passage to Canada and placed into homes for adoption. The practice started in the late 1860s and continued in different forms right up until the 1930s. At the time, it was believed that compulsory emigration would give these disadvantaged children a better life and a more solid moral upbringing than being raised on the city streets of England.

Most of these children were not, however, orphans. In fact, it is believed that of the thousands of children that came to Canada under this plan in the late Confederation era, only 2 percent were actually orphans. This was an era that had limited or non-existent social services, and the remainder were children put out for care by families who through poverty, illness, or some other affliction, could no longer support them.

The most famous of the organizations that sponsored such children was the Bernardo Home. Since then, the term "Bernardo Children" has come to be used as a generic name for all such children. However, more than fifty charities sent these children to Canada. The vast majority came from England, although there were some homes in Ireland and Scotland as well. Often, within a week of being placed in a charity, children would find themselves on board a steamer headed for Canada. The children would get off the ship in groups in Halifax or Montreal, usually with cardboard signs hanging about their necks identifying which charity they belonged to. They would then be

One of the home children at work on an Ontario farm.

collected at the pier by an administrative official and sent to a "distribution centre" where they would be sent by train to their new families to begin life anew in Canada.

For every boy or girl sent to Canada, there were seven applicants who wanted to adopt a child. Although in theory the practice sounded reasonable, many of the children found themselves placed not in loving homes but with families where they were put to work in harsh circumstances as unpaid farm hands or domestic servants. There are no statistics on how many children actually found a better situation, but anecdotal evidence indicates that the numbers who found themselves in abusive situations were far from insignificant. It was a system open to abuse, and there were no checks in place to make sure that the system worked as it was intended.

Chapter Twelve

THE IMMIGRANT PEOPLES:
THE ERA'S NEW MINORITIES

Although the aboriginal peoples, the French, and the British are often described as Canada's founding nations, by the time of the Confederation decades, minorities were already a significant part of the Canadian cultural montage.

Canada had several minority groups in its population, and Canadians of German ancestry were a significant one by 1840. The first German settlers came to Quebec as early as 1760, and were soon followed by Moravian missionaries in Labrador. Germans made up an estimated 15 percent of total United Empire Loyalist immigration, and later groups emigrated to Nova Scotia early in the nineteenth century. In the Confederation decades, there was large-scale migration to Ontario — most prominently, colonies of German-speaking Mennonites moved *en masse* from Pennsylvania to the Kitchener area. Subsequently, with the advent of the railway, very large numbers of Germans moved to the Prairies. German immigration in the Confederation era came mostly from the Danube Swabian communities in Hungary, Romania, and Serbia, as well as from Eastern Europe and the Austro-Hungarian Empire. Interestingly, the majority of German immigrants to Canada during the Confederation decades came from outside Germany itself. And migrants who came to North America from Germany tended to prefer the United States.

Germans of the Confederation era had few problems integrating within Canada's larger anglophone society. They intermarried freely and experienced no serious political, economic, or social restrictions. Their integration was so complete that they became an invisible minority.

Black Canadians have as long and distinguished a history as any European settlers. It is, however, a history marred by persecution and racial intolerance. The first recorded black Canadian came to New France as a slave as early as 1629. There were never large numbers of black slaves in Quebec.* However, there are records of slaves being imported overland from the American colonies primarily for domestic employment near the end of the seventeenth century. Although slaves were never imported to Quebec in great numbers, and no slave ship ever docked in Canada, the practice of slavery was not outlawed in Canada until 1834.

Loyalists brought slaves with them, but the majority of Loyalist blacks came as free men and women, having been freed by the British for fighting on behalf of the Crown. Nonetheless, some two thousand slaves arrived in British North America after the American Revolutionary War: five hundred were brought into Ontario, three hundred accompanied settlers to Quebec's Eastern Townships, and a further twelve hundred slaves came to New Brunswick, Nova Scotia, and Prince Edward Island.

By the Confederation era, slavery in Canada had only been recently abolished. It was a sensitive subject in British North America and across the Empire, and because of that, the abolition of slavery had to be done by degrees. The Slave Act was passed in 1793 in Upper Canada. It outlawed the import of slaves, and further stated that children born to slaves had to be freed on their twenty-fifth birthday. Trading slaves was outlawed in 1807, and ownership of slaves was abolished outright in 1834.

---

* Slavery in Quebec was never a common practice. However, there were occasional instances of aboriginal slaves who were taken prisoner during inter-tribal Indian wars and subsequently sold into slavery by local tribes.

The last black Canadian slave was a remarkable man, a Mr. John Baker. We know that he was given his freedom in 1804. Shortly thereafter, he served in the British Army, and was wounded in the War of 1812. He later fought at Waterloo and returned to Canada. Forty-five years after his service, he was finally awarded a military pension of a shilling a day. He died in Cornwall in 1871 at the age of a 104.[1]

Thousands of other blacks, before and during the American Civil War, came to Canada on the Underground Railroad as fugitive slaves. There was never an actual physical railway devoted for the use of escaped slaves, but those who ran the secret network used railway terminology as a secret code to prevent vital information from being intercepted by slave catchers. The network began as early as 1790, and some estimates place the number of slaves coming to Canada as high as thirty thousand. There is no certainty as there are no reliable records. Out of fear of being turned back to slave catchers claiming bogus criminal offences, blacks often did not register with the Canadian civil authorities. The numbers of former American slaves living in Canada was reduced after the Civil War and the emancipation of slaves, when many blacks chose to return to the U.S. to be reunited with their families.

Despite Canada's role in the Underground Railroad and despite the fact that slavery was abolished decades before, life for blacks in Canada remained extremely hard during the Confederation decades. They were denied housing, work, education, and other social and economic benefits. They were also denied leadership

Anxious to serve their new country, these men were denied entry to the volunteer fire department. Undeterred by the period's bigotry, they formed a black militia company, Victoria, 1862.

positions, even though they frequently distinguished themselves in military service.

One of the first Canadian military units ever to serve on the West Coast was an all-black militia unit, the Victoria Pioneer Rifle Corps. Anxious to serve their community, they created their own militia company in Victoria, B.C., after they were refused permission to join the new city's volunteer fire department.

Some early black Canadians did receive recognition. The first black Canadian to win a Victoria Cross (and the second-ever Canadian winner) was Able Seaman William Hall from Horton, Nova Scotia. Hall found himself attached to an artillery detachment of the British Army in India in 1857. During the siege of Lucknow in the Indian Mutiny, he single-handedly manned his field gun long after all his fellow gunners had been killed. His bravery was cited as one of the key actions that allowed for the successful storming of the city.

Canadians can be justifiably proud of their role in the Underground Railroad, but throughout the Confederation era, across the nation and across all nations of European descent, blacks were often treated unfairly. Despite having full protection and rights under Canadian laws, informal segregationist policies were frequently the norm in schools and public institutions; and until the mid-twentieth century, mainstream Canadian society inflicted routine and tacit discrimination on blacks in virtually all walks of life.

There were very few Asian Canadians during the Confederation decades. The first significant Asian migration to Canada took place on the West Coast. By 1850, with the discovery of gold in California, 50,000 Chinese, along with 300,000 other "gold diggers," had moved to California. In 1858, gold was again discovered — this time in the Fraser Valley — and by 1860, 7,000 Chinese had moved north to Vancouver Island and the B.C. mainland in search of Gum Shan (the gold mountain). Within five years, the gold rush was over, and with its end came increased resentment of Chinese labourers — men who were accustomed to working long hours for low wages. Once the European-Canadian majority decided that there was a threat of economic competition, the bitter sense of racial superiority and latent mistrust so pervasive in Victorian society bubbled to the surface. Chinese settlement in Canada was actively discouraged, and for twenty years, it all but died out.

Chinese immigration did not resume until cheap effective labour was needed to push the railway through from the Rockies to the Pacific. From 1880 to 1885, between ten to fifteen thousand Chinese workmen were brought into Canada. They dug, blasted, and hammered their way through eight hundred kilometres of rock and forest to complete the British Columbia section of the Canadian Pacific Railway. Working through the spring, summer, and fall for a dollar a day, less deductions for their rations and accommodation costs, and under the most appalling conditions, they drove the transcontinental railway through the successive chains of B.C.'s mountains. Landslides, exposure, preventable sickness, negligent use of explosives, fires, and other safety accidents claimed the lives of more than six hundred Chinese labourers. Accurate records were not kept, so we don't know precise numbers, but we do know the fatality rate was horrendous.

Further east, Chinese immigration and employment on the Canadian Pacific Railway caused a political uproar. Victorian Canadians were terrified that these men were the first of uncounted millions waiting to cross the Pacific, and believed that their European culture would rapidly be swamped by "hordes" of frantic Chinese. To examine the issue in 1884, Parliament convened a Royal Commission on Chinese Immigration. The result was the Chinese Immigration Act. It was Canada's first legislation that restricted immigration based on race. It didn't exclude all Chinese immigration, but it placed a $50 head tax on Chinese immigrants (a tax designed to be high enough to prevent Chinese men already in Canada from bringing their wives and families over). To further restrict mass migration, the bill limited ships to the transport of only one Chinese immigrant per fifty tons of cargo carried.*

---

* This restriction effectively limited the largest ships plying the Pacific shipping lanes to between 60 and 75 immigrants per ship.

Chinese men building the Canadian Pacific Railway, early 1880s.

In spite of the vindictiveness and humiliation of the Chinese Immigration Act, Chinese immigrants did come to Canada during the Confederation era and they left the country with three invaluable legacies. First, without their extraordinary efforts, the transcontinental railway would certainly not have been completed in anything like the time it was; second, what is now British Columbia might well have had an American flag flying over it; and third, every Canadian town on the national line has reaped the benefits of having a Chinese community grow up in it.

Despite their enormously beneficial impact on almost every aspect of Canadian life, Jewish migration to Canada has always been relatively small scale. Jews have settled in Canada since the earliest days of European settlement. However, Jews have always been just a tiny fraction of Canada's population, numbering only 451 people in 1851, and just under two thousand by the close of the Confederation era. During this period, most Jews arriving in Canada came from Germanic countries or Britain. Their numbers would increase somewhat, near the turn of the century, with the migration of Ashkenazi Jews fleeing pogroms in Eastern Europe.

Migration of many of Canada's other sizeable minorities did not happen until after the Confederation era and well into the twentieth century. Ukrainians, Italians, South Asians, Arabs, Poles, Scandinavians, Persians, East Europeans, and Hispanics came to Canada in large numbers well after the West was settled, and, more significantly, once the government — and the Canadian people — developed sufficient confidence to accept people with markedly diverse cultural backgrounds. The experiences of the Confederation era made that acceptance possible.

Chapter Thirteen

RURAL LIFE

Throughout the Confederation decades, Canada was primarily a nation with an agriculturally based economy, and the vast majority of its farms were small, family-run holdings. During this period, most of these farms gradually evolved from being subsistence-level operations to more profitable and sophisticated operations. As farming improved, surplus agricultural output grew, and as production increased, rural populations became an increasingly important political force.

Agricultural improvements during the era were the result of several factors. Agriculture itself was becoming a more specialized occupation. With the growth of mass manufacturing and higher education levels, farm machinery and farming methods were improved appreciably each year. With more and better railways and a growing road network, heavier machinery could be transported to more remote areas. As a result, newer, heavier ploughs, reapers, mowers, and threshers came

into common use, and farmers could cultivate much larger acreages — all of which increased national agricultural yields.

Nonetheless, during the Confederation era, the standard of living on farms varied considerably. In areas that were being settled, it was not unusual to find farm families living, at least in the early years of their homesteading, in conditions that would have been the norm for settlers just before the War of 1812. This was despite the fact that, during the four core decades of the Confederation era, farming methods and equipment improved by leaps and bounds. For example, single-sided ploughing, which used the old, single-bladed ploughshare traditionally pulled by an ox or a horse, gave way to ploughing with self-sharpening, multiple-furrow ploughs. These were later replaced by circular-disc ploughs that were made out of much higher quality steel. By 1880, most farms in Ontario,

Quebec, and the Atlantic provinces were operating on a par with their counterparts in Europe and the more settled areas of the United States; but it was still not unusual for new settlers who had little money to use the methods and the machinery of a previous generation.

As farming methods improved, farm lifestyles began to change as well. Yet throughout this period, the underlying farm culture in Canada remained fairly constant. The major cultural shifts in rural Canadian society were still several decades away. Farm and village life would not undergo a major transformation until the First World War.

One of the distinguishing constants of farmers in all the countries of the New World was that for them it was vitally important to own their own land. Unlike Europe, where farmers tended to be tenants on properties owned

The first trickle of East European immigrants began in the Confederation decades. They were followed in later years by a flood of hardworking and capable farmers. These Austro-Hungarian women are on a hardscrabble Ontario farm in the early 1880s.

by members of an upper class, Canadian farmers, even if they were poor and struggling, were landowners; and with freehold ownership came a different and more independent outlook. Canadian farmers did not view themselves as an underclass. They saw themselves as dignified, self-sufficient, and independent. Paying rent for farmland was not considered to be shameful, but it was not what families aspired to. Independent land ownership was a key attraction and a source of intense pride. To achieve ownership, even during the more technologically developed later years of the era, new homesteaders would willingly live much like the early pioneers, with few comforts, considerable hardship, and tremendous risks.

Risks of many different kinds were a constant factor in the lives of Confederation-era farmers. Weather, crop and animal diseases, sickness, or injury could be critical factors in the success and prosperity of a family farm. One year a farmer could find himself with bumper crops and surplus income, and the next they could be plunged into hunger, debt, and poverty. As in Ireland and Scotland, potato blight in the late 1840s and early 1850s forced many farm families off the land or into penury. Frosts, droughts, and insect infestations were common and caused near-famine conditions in many areas. New settlers with small farms and limited livestock herds were particularly vulnerable. In many cases, the smaller landholders were the ones seeking additional employment in nearby towns or in the timber business.

The poorest settlers were those in the newly settled areas. They lived closest to the land and built log or sod houses. They had few comforts or amenities. In the more-established areas, farm houses were much more elaborate and comfortable, usually well-furnished, and often built from quarried stone, brick, or timber. In the 1840s, it was not unusual for pioneer settlers to live in traditional log cabins. Those first houses and out buildings would most frequently be built in a matter of days with the assistance of nearby community members. Most often, the buildings on these farms were temporary ones, usually only a single-storey hut, a square metre or two, with an angled lean-to–like roof. In the early years, doors would be slabs of timber, often on leather hinges, and windows would be simple openings covered by a rough shutter. Fireplaces were made from stone and chimneys were built from mud, stones, and sticks. Fires were not uncommon, and in winter they were often fatal.

The earliest farm houses were drafty, cold, crowded, and unsanitary. If a dirt floor was not used, the houses' first floors were made from roughhewn timbers. Furniture might consist of a homemade bench, a simple table, and a shelf or two to hold whatever pots and utensils were on hand. When a farmer first built his house, one side would often be reserved for his family, and if he had time before winter, the other side for his animals. By the second year, a farmer would have assembled a second shelter and perhaps a corn crib to store his crops: corn, wheat, hay and any root vegetables that he had grown. Perhaps by the third year, if things had gone well, he would build a separate livestock barn. All these out-buildings would have been carefully positioned so that they provided the farmhouse a break from the prevailing wind.

Most farmers' standard of living improved dramatically in the first decade on the land. Confederation-era settlers were industrious people, with a work ethic that today might be regarded as compulsive. Throughout the year, they worked day in and day out and their farms improved quickly. Occasionally, some farmers would remain in the original building as a means of paying reduced taxes, but most quickly added larger structures to those first houses or turned them into barns or animal shelters.

As farm houses improved, one of the first purchases farmers made during the Confederation decades was a new iron stove. Stoves came in many sizes and degrees of complexity. Their great advantage was that they were infinitely more efficient than open fires, used less fuel, and distributed heat much more evenly. Farm stoves made heating, cooking, and laundry chores much easier. They also meant that different kinds of meals could be prepared, and in this respect they not only contributed to comfort and convenience, but they made the farmers' diet more varied and interesting. The growth of iron mining in North America in the 1820s led to the development of precast, multi-purpose iron stoves. The first stoves in Canada were imported from Britain, but later were manufactured in the same foundries in Quebec and Ontario that built steamboat engines for the Great Lakes.

In addition to heat, easy access to water was equally critical for survival on a Confederation-era farm. There were two methods that farmers used to procure adequate supplies of water. The first and simplest was to draw fresh water from a natural source such as a stream, creek, or river. However, most new farms were established some distance from existing watercourses and farmers had to dig wells. Since biblical time, wells had been hand dug and lined with either stones or bricks to keep them from collapsing. Most farm wells in Canada were dug by hand; however, in the 1830s, some wells were dug mechanically with a kind of iron boring post operated by a horse plodding along a circular track. Steam drills did not come into common use in Canada until the 1890s. In the later years of the era, wells were outfitted with galvanized iron pipes.

Dowsing or divining for water on farms was a fairly common practice throughout the Confederation era. Although, the typical dowser with a hazel or willow rod searching for water had no scientific basis, most professional water diviners had a well-developed sense as to where the water table lay. Wells typically would be dug near underground springs and streams that fed nearby watercourses — and it was not uncommon to dig numerous dry wells before finding a viable water source.

Although farmers might occasionally rely upon outside help for unique tasks — like locating a well — Confederation-era farmers were a self-reliant group and performed almost all of the work that needed doing on their farms themselves. Most of this generation of farmers were incredibly skilled people; and although we often consider their time a less sophisticated one than ours, we would do well to consider the range of skills these men and women had. Not only did they grow and prepare all their food, but they also built and repaired almost everything they owned. Farmers always had a collection of tools on hand for doing any and all repairs.

Beside the barn, or next to the farmhouse, was often a small shed with the farmer's tools: a carpenter's bench, a vise, hammers, numerous saws, planes, chisels, perhaps a wood lathe, and woodworking tools with which they fashioned shingles, plough handles, oxen and horse yokes, leather work of every description, furniture, toys, and the bits and pieces required to repair a thousand broken or worn out items.

Despite their ingrained self-reliance, farmers all across Canada frequently relied on each other. Indeed, there was a communal aspect to Confederation-era rural life that has almost entirely died out in modern society. Across the country, it was not uncommon for neighbours to assist one another on projects, often devoting weeks at a time to an activity. It was a shared, freely provided kind of interdependence among neighbours that is almost alien to modern sensibilities. One such tradition that has all but disappeared in our times is the barn-raising bee.

Barn raising was a shared, voluntary, community effort where people came together to build or repair an individual's barn. Barns were immense structures. They were the period's largest element of rural infrastructure and were an essential part of every farm. The energy and time required to build one was completely beyond the means of any one family, and so each family relied on the larger community to help them. Even with an entire community's help, building one was a daunting task, especially for a novice farmer.

Barn raisings became a characteristic part of life. No debts were incurred for the community's work. No one was ever paid for their services, and virtually everyone in a community was expected to volunteer when a barn had to go up. Petty grievances and personal squabbles were put aside as everyone pitched in to get the work done. Barns could not be built without the efforts of hundreds of men and their families working together for the one or two days it took to get them put up. However, the preparation that went into raising a barn would often take a year or more of backbreaking effort and scrupulous planning.

Months before the actual day of the barn raising, farmers would plan the location, size, and layout of the building. In an era before cranes or any sort of heavy-duty engineering equipment, barn design and planning was a task requiring unique skills, aptitude, and ingenuity. There were few architects or professional builders in rural Canada, and planning for the barn's design was usually a group effort drawing upon the expertise of several men. The year before the barn was built, the owner of the new barn would seek the advice of several experienced community members. The most knowledgeable barn builder would usually be designated as the foreman. Once a design had been agreed upon, trees would be felled, timber cut and milled, pegs and dowels carved, buckets of nails forged, stone foundations built, ropes prepared and coiled, beams and planks numbered, notched, and marked, and all the additional materials carefully laid out days before the community descended on the farm.

Most barns were erected within a day or two in June or July. These months allowed farmers sufficient time to do the job between planting and harvest, and the weather would likely be favourable. Women in the

A large, well-to-do family with servants on the lawn of their house. Eastern Townships, Quebec, mid-1860s.

community worked for days baking and preparing enormous quantities of food: roasts of beef and lamb, chickens, venison, pies, breads, and salads, as well as quantities of cider, beer, and tea. When the barn was up, it was traditional to hold a dance in the new building.

Barn raisings knitted communities closer together, and because people had to get along, they served as a means of ensuring civility and respect within the community.

In addition to the man-made infrastructure of the Confederation-era farm, the land itself took considerable care and attention. For a settler, clearing the land was an enormous task. This was a time before the chainsaw, and removing the trees from a section of farmland was a staggering task. In New France, farmers with an axe could clear an acre and a half a year. By 1840, with better saws and improved animal harnesses, Canadian farmers could manage four to five acres a year.

Once the trees were felled, farmers had to deal with the issue of stumps. Stumping was a huge problem. You could not effectively plough a field full of stumps. Left to itself to rot away, a hardwood stump might take fifty years to disintegrate before it could be ploughed over. Confederation-era farmers got rid of their stumps in several ways: controlled burns, pulling them with a team of oxen, and massive, purpose-built, stump-pulling tools that made use of a screw-type device and a horse that uprooted the stump. Stumps pulled from the ground with their star shaped web of roots were often laid side-by-side and used as highly effective fencing.

Much later in the era, dynamite was used to get rid of stumps. Dynamite, effectively positioned, made short work of the most massive stumps. However,

Clearing fields of stones and stumps remained a major undertaking in the Confederation decades. Here, farmers use a modified buckboard and levers to move a granite boulder from a farm field in 1870s Ontario.

there was one serious problem with dynamite — it required great skill to use. Dynamite could be bought relatively cheaply in a general store, but few farmers were trained in its use. Horrific farm accidents with dynamite were commonplace.

Though dynamite had replaced the use of oxen in stumping by the late 1860s, it would be some time before animals were replaced on farms more generally. Indeed, one of the major differences between Confederation-era farmers and modern farmers was their dependence on animals as a source of mechanical work. In the early Confederation decades, oxen were one of the most common animals used by farmers. Oxen (castrated male cattle) were used for their size and strength to pull and haul things such as ploughs or heavy wagons.

Confederation-era farmers found oxen useful for several reasons. An ox's horns continue to grow throughout its life, which means that the animal is able to develop a wide spread of horns, which helps to keep their yokes from slipping off their heads. As well, oxen have a more reliable temperament than horses or mules, the two other most common farm utility animals of the period. Oxen are generally steadier and more consistent out in a farm field, and are less likely to bolt when startled. Oxen also have the added practical benefit that when their useful mechanical life is over, they can be eaten. However, oxen tend to live shorter lives than horses or mules. Oxen live for about ten years, compared to an average twenty-year lifespan for horses, and thirty-five years for mules.

However, largely for reasons of economy, oxen were initially the more popular animals in Canada. While horses can move much faster than oxen, they are also much more expensive to feed. And, unlike oxen, horses, for cultural reasons, have rarely been eaten by Canadians. Despite all these advantages and disadvantages, horses were consistently the more common draft animal in the United States during this period.

As the design of farm equipment improved throughout the Confederation era, teams of horses were increasingly used instead of oxen. With the advent of multi-bladed ploughs and discs, using a team of horses meant a farmer could cultivate far more ground and thereby drastically increase the productivity of his farm. Mules, on the other hand, which are the sterile offspring of a male donkey and a mare, are far more intelligent, stronger for their size, and more patient than horses, but because they could not be bred, they were never widely used in Canada.

Canadian horses played a significant role in the American Civil War. Canada bred several large, reliable varieties of horses, and sold tens of thousands of them to the Union Army for use as artillery draft horses and cavalry mounts. Without a steady supply of these strong, dependable horses, the Northern war effort would have been seriously hampered. But it was not just the horse breeding business that did well during the Civil War. Farming in general in Canada benefitted enormously from a lucrative export trade, as the North imported large quantities of Canadian food stuffs throughout the conflict.

Another key element of rural life that has all but disappeared today was the rural mill. Mills played an overlooked but important role in the Confederation-era's rural economy. Mills of all sorts ground grain, cut wood, and spun wool, and they were a common feature of the Canadian rural landscape. In eastern Canada, mills were most often built on rivers, and tended to be, as in early Quebec, situated within a day's wagon ride from farming communities. Because farmers travelling to a mill needed a place to eat and sleep, towns and villages frequently grew up around the mill. Since farmers brought their produce in wagons, livery stables and blacksmith shops also sprang up close to the mill, as did general stores, churches, and schools.

In western Canada, small mills did not play as critical a role in the development of the region, as railways brought grain to larger industrial-scale mills. Instead of the mill, the predominant feature of a prairie village was the grain elevator. Grain elevators did not come into use until very late in the Confederation period, with the first ones being purpose-built in Manitoba in 1879. They soon became a characteristic feature of every village.

A standard establishment in Confederation-era rural villages was the country general store. The general store was more than simply a retail outlet that sold a wide variety of goods, and the store owner and his wife were much more than just retail clerks. The store owner was a man of considerable importance and power. His store was one of the most important institutions in rural society. Not only was it a store, it also served as a social focal point. People would gather at the store when in town to exchange gossip and information. It also served as the post office, and, in some cases, the telegraph office. And for the community's hired hands, those single men who worked seasonally on the farms and often had no other place to go than a bunk house to socialize, it became the only alternative to the tavern.

The general storekeeper was a man of considerable economic importance in early Confederation-era rural life. The storekeeper decided whether or not to extend credit to farmers who needed his goods, but were unable to pay until they sold their harvest in the autumn. As a creditor, the storekeeper was common right across the country. In Newfoundland, the general store bought the catches and set the prices for cod and seal. In the Maritimes, Quebec, Ontario, the Prairies, and British Columbia, the storekeeper not only extended credit, but determined what kinds of goods would be available. In many ways, they became the arbiters of fashion and taste in a rural community, as all store-bought clothing, spices, sugar, hand tools, medicines, tea, coffee, dry goods, hardware, textiles, and glass came across the storekeeper's counter.

Rural life in Canada during the Confederation decades certainly entailed hardship and privation, but in comparison to much of the rest of the world, Canadian farmers and their families lived well. The climate was certainly harsh and unforgiving, the work was exacting and unending, but the soils were generally fertile, food was abundant, the country was at peace, and, despite the changes of the period, life was settled, reassuringly predictable, and rewarding.

An early general store in the B.C. interior. This one was notable for being owned and managed by recent Chinese immigrants. General stores of the period often served as druggists and post offices — a phenomenon that seems to be repeating itself in twenty-first-century Canada.

Chapter Fourteen

URBAN LIFE

In 1867, only 17 percent of Canadians lived in cities. This differed significantly from Britain at the time, where more than half the population lived in cities, and lagged well behind the United States, where 25 percent of the population lived in urban areas. Still, cities and towns were becoming more numerous and larger, and they played an increasingly important role as the era progressed.

Modern Canadians would not be unfamiliar with large sections of many Confederation-era cities. The downtown core areas of several cities still have period buildings that are more than a hundred and fifty years old, and the street layouts are unchanged. The most striking difference between Confederation era cities and modern ones would not be the buildings, but the number of horses on the street. It would be hard to underestimate the horse's effect on Canada's Victorian cities.

The character of cities, which were populated with thousands of horses serving as the prime sources of motive power, was drastically different from what we know today. Horses had a profound impact on urban life. The logistics of maintaining large numbers of horses not only influenced the pace and rhythm of life, but it largely defined the character of Canada's urban areas.

The horses used in Canada's cities were generally immense animals, often weighing more than nine hundred kilos. To keep a working horse of that size properly fed meant that it was eating in the order of eight thousand litres of oats and six-and-a-half large, round dry bales of grassy hay each year. Horses also had a tremendous environmental impact: each horse left around ten kilos of manure and a litre of urine on the city streets every day. In some cities today you can still find an occasional horse-drawn cab, such as the tourist carriages found in Quebec City or Victoria, and the waste left by those animals on the streets presents no real problem. However, in the Confederation era, when

Traffic congestion is not just a modern problem. Horses and carriages at the market in Quebec City, early 1870s.

Canada's cities were filled with thousands of horses in dense city centres, the waste produced by these animals became an enormous health hazard.

In small numbers, horses could pose a serious health problem, but on busy streets the mounds of rotting manure that they left attracted clouds of house flies and other pests, which were also additional deadly vectors for infectious diseases. Cold weather provided little relief. When it rained or when the snow melted, unpaved city streets turned into an unhealthy paste several centimetres thick. In dry weather, the streets became extremely dusty, and pedestrians, after even a short walk, would routinely be covered from head to foot in a bacterially rich coating of dust.

The horses employed in Canada's cities lived brief and unpleasant existences. The average draft horse in North American cities was overworked and had a commercial life expectancy of about four years.[1] This was substantially different than the nineteenth century twenty-year average lifespan for farm horses. Horses in the city were mistreated by brutal and negligent drivers and teamsters who, in the interest of short-term profit, often worked their animals to death. Complaints of reckless driving of horse teams were common, and gruesome accidents between large teams of horses were an everyday occurrence. In winter, when roads were icy, tired, iron-shod horses would often slip and break a leg, and suffering animals would have to be put down in the street. Because of their weight and size, dead horses created a significant problem. With the technology of the day, it was difficult to move them, and it was not uncommon in Canada's cities of the Confederation era to have a dead work horse left in the street for days on end.

Transportation evolved significantly in Canada's cities during the Confederation decades. By the mid-1860s, several Canadian cities had horse-drawn streetcars. Streetcars were a huge improvement in Canada's growing cities. Prior to their introduction, most urban travellers either hired or took their own carriage, or more commonly walked. Both options were extremely inconvenient. Walking along the city's filthy streets was usually an unpleasant chore, and one had to be reasonably well-to-do to hire a private carriage. If you were staying any length of time, horse drawn carriages, even simple pony traps or buggies that held one or two people, normally had to be attended to when you arrived at your destination. Leaving horses unattended on the street for long periods was not advisable, as horse theft was a common crime. Horses were an inconvenient mode of transport as they needed to be fed, watered, and rested frequently. Often, if a journey required more than a few minutes at the other end, unless you could stable your horses securely, you had to travel with someone who could look after your horse.

Streetcars, once they were introduced, quickly became popular, as they provided a convenient and comfortable alternative to walking and carriages. Toronto's first streetcar replaced an "omnibus service," which today we would call a stagecoach. The new streetcar ran every ten minutes from the St. Lawrence Market to Yorkville. As big an improvement as streetcars were, they only ran on very specific main routes and there were few connecting lines, which often meant that at least part of a trip still had to be made on foot.

While Confederation-era Canadians had to endure streets that were less than hygienic, the buildings that lined their streets were often built with a passion and a sense of flair — but it was a flair that was imported. Apart from the very old parts of Quebec City and Montreal, Canadian cities and towns during the Confederation decades looked similar to many American or British towns. That there was not a distinct Canadian architectural style is almost certainly because Canadian architects were initially trained either in Britain or the United States. The first school of architecture in Canada did not open until 1890 at the University of Toronto.

The two most popular architectural styles for public buildings during the Confederation decades were Classicism, a style that deliberately imitated Greek and Roman art, and Gothic Revival, with its arched windows and irregular appearance. The Classicists were most strongly influenced by the Italian Palladian school, which attempted to reproduce the temple architecture of the ancient Greeks and Romans. Across Canada, one can see numerous court houses, banks, and churches that were built during the Confederation era using central domes and temple-style columns. Less grand buildings, such as police and train stations, libraries, and even country stores, also often incorporated elements of this architectural style. But perhaps the best known architectural style of the period, and one that was enthusiastically embraced by Canadian builders, was that of the Gothic Revival.

Canada's Parliament buildings, period university buildings, as well as numerous Anglican and Catholic churches were all created as stunning examples of Gothic Revivalism. Strongly influenced by the ornate and sweeping lines of medieval buildings, this style, like the Classical style, harkened back to another age. Its use can be seen as an attempt to transfer to the new country a feeling of history, tradition, and character that a frontier society with deep roots in European tradition needed to strengthen its legitimacy.

Many Canadian houses from the Confederation period that we now often classify as "Victorian" combine elements of Classicism and Gothic Revival. People right across the country, English and French, from the Maritimes and the Prairies, built brick, stone, and wood

A Confederation-era streetcar in Ottawa, winter 1871.

houses incorporating both steeply pitched gables and verandas fronted by stately columns. With a characteristic Victorian obsession for detail, they edged many of their houses with gingerbread trim, ornamental molding, and protruding, Italianate eaves. For good measure, they frequently added stained glass to their hallways and larger rooms.

Smaller commercial buildings in Canada's towns and cities had a characteristic period style, much of it imported from Britain, but also from the eastern United States. Similar functional, box-like, red-brick commercial buildings, often with bay fronts in the top stories and large windows on the ground floor, can be seen today in every part of the country. Factories and industrial buildings were often, at least in some of the added details, indebted to the Gothic Revival tradition.

Many of the breweries, foundries, and factories were built as massive brick boxes. Some in the early years of the period incorporated the use of cast iron in their building frames; later, in the 1870s, the use of rolled steel in buildings became popular. In many commercial buildings of the period there was a flair and sense of elegance that today would be considered frivolous. True to their generation, some of them integrated into their design arched windows, herringbone infills, corbelled cornices, and even the occasional crenellated parapet. Most of the factories have long since been torn down, but in the downtown core of Canada's small towns, many smaller retail and commercial buildings still provide a sense of what once was ordinary.

From the mid-1840s, the wealthy tended to move out to more exclusive enclaves that were well away from urban factories, wharves, and warehouses. The industrial areas of Canadian cities initially tended to be along the waterfronts; later, they were built further back and along the newly constructed railways that ran through the cities. Shops, professional offices, and artisanal manufacturing were clustered in the traditional town centres. Middle-class residential areas in the Confederation era were closer to the town centre than today's suburbs.

Houses in Canadian cities ran the gamut from being very large palatial residences of the well-heeled, upper and upper-middle classes to cramped drafty townhouses.

The houses of the well-to-do were meant to be impressive. Inherited wealth was not as common nor as prestigious as in Britain; and in Canada's cities the

Grocery shopping, Montreal market, late 1870s.

self-made man whose wealth came from commerce, the professions, and industry was not shy about displaying his status and affluence. There was certainly a Calvinist streak in Victorian Canada, and earned wealth was regarded as a sign of character, while poverty was viewed as a personal shortcoming. Ostentatious but suitably gracious living was expected of the wealthy. Upper-class Canadians, both English and French, tended in different degrees to follow the manners and traditions of wealthy English families. Consequently, Toronto, Montreal, Quebec, Halifax, Saint John, and all the growing towns along the St. Lawrence watershed had neighbourhoods with magnificently impressive homes.

Confederation-era homes came in a variety of styles, the most common styles being Queen Anne Revival, Georgian, Gothic, and Colonial Revival.

The homes of the wealthiest often had a dozen or more bedrooms to accommodate large Victorian families. Victorian Canadian upper-class families needed numerous bedrooms because they almost always came with numerous children, maiden aunts, elderly parents, and frequent house guests. Most of their houses had a large wood-panelled front hallway with a sweeping front stairway, as well as a smaller, much more functional, discrete set of back stairs for the servants. There would be a large kitchen near the back stairs, several drawing rooms, a formal dining room, and often a well-appointed study where the man of the house could retire when he sought privacy. Grander Victorian city houses in the most popular Queen Anne Revival tradition often included a tower or enclosed turret, with a narrow staircase leading to a small room used for reading, painting, or private contemplation. Most had broad, wraparound porches kitted out with wicker furniture. Few had real basements, but almost all had cellars that were used for storage, and, if built after the late 1850s, they would likely contain a coal furnace. Earlier houses that did not have central heating had small fireplaces in most rooms.

A wealthy city household would have had a large carriage house and an attached stable. Gardens for Canada's wealthier classes in the city might not be large, but they would be well tended by servants or professional gardeners. Gardens were usually planted with hardwood trees, a lawn, perennial flowers, shrubs, and, where possible, hedges to provide privacy from passersby.

Middle-class houses in Canadian cities and towns were invariably more modest. The most popular house built during the period was the simple, rectangular "Gothic cottage," with a centre gable that usually jutted out over the front door. It was first designed in the late eighteenth century, and in one form or another was the most commonly built style of separate house in Canada until after Second World War.[2] These storey-and-a-half houses were common to cities and to rural areas. They were simple to build, the upper half-storey retained heat in the winter, and, for much of the Confederation period in Ontario, these houses were taxed at a lower rate than normal full two-storey buildings. As families became more affluent, it was common to put an addition at the back, in either an L or a T shape, often with an expanded second storey.

Middle-class houses in urban areas were by no means standardized in terms of size, aesthetics, function, or value. The middle class in the Confederation era was as amorphous as it is today, as most urban Canadians of the time considered themselves to belong to this group.

Middle-income Canadians lived just beyond the city centre. The poorer groups, who had to walk the furthest through the city's grubby streets, tended to live toward the margins of the city, a situation that would not change appreciably until the automobile came into general use.

Many middle-class families had a servant or two, as did farm families, who frequently had hired hands living with them. Having domestic help was not considered to be a key social differentiator. For most, it was a practical necessity in an age where household chores were much more labour intensive than they are now.

Maids, cooks, serving girls, and domestic day labourers were common in Confederation-era Canada. The further up the social ladder one rose, the larger one's house would be, and, correspondingly, the greater the number of servants one would have. But as we shall see subsequently, class differences in Canada, while they certainly existed, were not nearly as pronounced as they were in Britain or the deep south of the United States.

There were few large apartment buildings in any of the Canadian cities during the Confederation decades. Most of the urban working classes lived in townhouses. The townhouse was largely a British influence, and, until its wide-scale adoption in Canada in the mid-1800s, most people, including the poor, lived in detached houses. Townhouses were, in the early years of their adoption, very much a lower-middle- and working-class dwelling. Few residents of townhouses would have had servants, although in many cases, to make ends meet, boarders might live with a family.

The typical townhouse built in the late 1840s, as, for example, those in Montreal, had a flat-roof and was a two-storey brick or wooden structure. The downstairs typically consisted of a hallway, a staircase, a tiny sitting room and space for a dining table and a kitchen. Upstairs, there was one or two bedrooms. They were small, but not nearly as crowded and cramped as the tenement apartments that had become standard during this period for immigrants in America's northern cities. The likely explanation for Canadian cities of the period not adopting tenement-type apartment blocks was not that landlords were more generous in Canada, or had any greater sense of obligation to the tenant, but that Canadian house builders were slower in adopting cast-iron framing as a building technique. Cast iron was cheaper, quicker to build with, and allowed the builder to put up much taller structures that could house more people.

By the early 1850s in many Canadian cities, the problems of urban hygiene began to recede. The introduction of municipal sewers and water distribution systems were the most important health and safety innovations in Canada's history. The earliest water systems were introduced in Saint John and Halifax, with Ontario and Quebec following suit within a decade. Even with the new technology, health improvements were gradual. It would often take a decade or more to install water and sewer systems across an entire city. The projects were expensive and labour intensive and took years to install. As a result, for most of the Confederation period, people used privies or outhouses.

Privies in most urban areas were dug to a depth of five or six feet, and in the case of townhouse communities, they were invariably sited in the back of a tiny yard. When the old privies filled up, there was little room to dig a new one and having them emptied was expensive. Consequently, tenants did not re-site or clear them as frequently as hygiene and fragrance demanded. For this reason, the areas behind Confederation-era townhouses were rarely cultivated as gardens or used as backyard retreats.

No matter the class of people using them, privies had several problems associated with their use. Privies filled up, and they had to be emptied by men who hauled away the "night soil" — a euphemism based on the fact that these unfortunate men almost always did their work at night. Using buckets and barrels, they carted their loads away while their fellow citizens slept. In many cities, trenches were dug for depositing night soil outside the city limits. However, because of the late hours and the distances, night soil collectors often dumped their barrels in the nearest watercourse; or, when no one was looking and they could get away with it, they jettisoned their cargo onto vacant city lots. Being a night soil collector was not a prestigious occupation and prim Victorian Canadians either ignored them or scorned them as society's "scavengers."

The problems of waste management were vastly different than what we have become accustomed to in the twenty-first century. Before the introduction of sewers, there were several attempts at finding alternative ways of dealing with waste. The City of Montreal, for example, experimented for several years with using "destructors," an innovative system of burning the city's night soil. But with the introduction of sewers, the project was abandoned.

Before the advent of sewers, people for centuries grew up with different smells and different standards and thought little of it. In the same manner, both in the cities and in the country, people were not as conscious of the problems of bacterial contamination, and for convenience sake, often sited their privies close to their houses and wells. In a climate with extremely cold winters, people were reluctant to place the privy too far from the house. The result was that human waste regularly contaminated drinking water, and cholera, diphtheria, typhoid fever, intestinal parasites, and chronic gastrointestinal illnesses were, by today's standards, fairly common.

The issue of waste disposal was also connected with the presence of lanes, or alleys, in cities across Canada. Although some urban neighborhoods in the Confederation era had lanes behind their backyards, many did not. Municipal lanes, or alleys, began to become common in the 1840s. And in the early years of the twentieth century, lanes eventually became a feature of many middle-class neighborhoods, especially in western Canada. There was a practical aspect to having a lane behind one's house; there was also a unique touch of Canadian snobbery. Although class divisions in Canada were not as acute as elsewhere, they certainly existed. The lane as it was devised in the late Confederation era was originally designed to keep tradesmen, particularly night soil collectors, away from the front entrances of the houses of the well-to-do.

The introduction of sewers meant there was a substantial improvement in the sanitary conditions in Canada's cities and towns, but modern sewers also created serious problems. Sewers of the era were designed to send large quantities of raw sewage into the nearest body of water. Rivers, streams, and lakes soon became contaminated, and new and unforeseen environmental problems grew up, especially along the shores of Lake Ontario and in the St. Lawrence River near Montreal. Despite this, environmental and conservation efforts were not considered to be major problems for another sixty years.

Garbage disposal, on the other hand, did not present anything like the scale of the problem we are faced with today. Confederation-era Canadians were frugal people, and the actual amount of bulk waste they produced was far less than what modern Canadians throw out. Packaging was simpler, and much of what they did not reuse or compost they burned in their stoves. Garbage collection in Canada started in earnest in Toronto in the 1860s after a cholera outbreak. At the time, Toronto was considered by many to be one of the dirtiest cities in North America.

The tipping point was reached in about thirty years, by which time scientific understanding of the nature of diseases translated into actionable political opinion. Thousands of animals were slaughtered every year in the city, and the offal was dumped into the city's sewers, which drained into Lake Ontario and contaminated the city's drinking water, resulting in periodic epidemics. It was a time with a much different perspective and slower communications. Reaching the tipping point, when scientific understanding of the nature of infectious diseases translated into actionable political opinion, took about thirty years. The first boards of health in Canada were established in Ontario in 1882, and it would not be until later in the decade that municipal officials began to acknowledge the connection between bacterial infection and disease. Once simple water filtration systems were installed in most Canadian cities by the late nineteenth century, the mortality rate plummeted. It dropped even further when chlorination systems came on-line in the early twentieth century.

The other major change in the quality of urban life during the Confederation era was brought about by the introduction of gas lighting. Montreal was the first Canadian city to introduce a gas system in 1837. Toronto followed suit four years later, and by the early 1850s, gas was in use in most Canadian cities. Gas for lighting Canada's cities came principally from the gasification of coal, a procedure that turned coal into gas by a controlled process of infusing solid coal at high temperatures with oxygen and steam without causing combustion. Gas street lights were mounted around cities on high wooden posts, with the burners surrounded by white glass globes. These globes had to be manually lit and needed constant cleaning. Early use of gas lamps indoors was extremely expensive, and in many municipalities and homes, oil lamps provided a viable competitor to gas right up to the introduction of electricity in the 1890s. Initially, gas was confined to public spaces, such as hotels and railway stations, but it was soon put to use as outdoor illumination on city streets.

Fewer than 17 percent of Confederation-era Canadians lived in urban areas. The overwhelming rural character of the country was also inevitably reflected to some extent in the provincial feel of its cities and towns. Even with such modern innovations as gas light, sewers, modern architecture, and public transportation, Canada's urban areas remained charmingly unsophisticated. By comparison to the much larger, dirtier, more heavily industrialized, and more frantic metropolises of Britain and America, Canadian municipalities still had a quiet, measured, and almost rustic atmosphere. This small-town feel was due in part to the peaceful, egalitarian nature of the country; in part to the unpretentious nature of

Owen Sound, Ontario, gas lighting, and high fashion, 1870s.

a frontier society; and in part because the country still had one foot firmly planted in a pre-industrial era. All of these factors helped to give the country its unique, unaffected, nineteenth-century charm. Likewise, Canada's Confederation-era towns and cities had a delightful, unapologetically provincial charm to them. They were to keep that quality until well into in the twentieth century.

Chapter Fifteen

DOMESTIC LIFE

Domestic life in the Confederation era was in many ways uniquely Canadian. The nature of the family was changing more slowly than in other societies. Roles within the family were shifting gradually, and the manner in which people celebrated the significant events in their lives had become more complex, more elaborate, and, in some ways, considerably more bizarre than they had ever been.

Domestic life had moved from the simple and practical dictates of a pioneering ethos to a more self-assured culture, one seemingly bound by strict conventions and a stern Victorian code of manners and morality.

Canada was in the process of transforming from a frontier society to a hybridized nation, one that was overwhelmingly rural and traditional, but at the same time was adjusting to the onset of industrialization. The country had a world view that was in many ways dissimilar to America's industrialized northern states or Victorian Britain. As a society, Canada had not begun to industrialize on a large scale. The repercussions of the social problems and disparities that afflicted Britain's manufacturing cities, and the massive trauma of America's Civil War and its sudden industrialization, were all experienced vicariously in Canada. At the same time, Canadians were coming to grips with the fact that the wider world was changing and going through a period of major social and industrial transition.

Canada was a literate society and its people were well-aware of the new ideas and the shifting social structure of the times. It was also a country strongly influenced by large-scale migration from both America and Britain. As a result, many of the changed attitudes in the "old countries" were bound to show up in Canada, even if they did so in slightly different forms.

Most Canadian families lived in a growing rural society that had only recently become prosperous. Although

A married couple in Halifax, 1868. To keep their subjects still, photographers often tried posing them reading and staring with blank expressions. Slow shutter speeds and crude photographic plates caused blurring with the slightest motion. They also left future generations with the incorrect impression that their ancestors were stern and chronically morose.

meant that rural Canadians were relatively isolated and limited in their day-to-day range of personal contacts. Members of communities grew up, lived, and died knowing the same range of families and acquaintances throughout their lives. The practical alternatives available to men and women in choosing a life partner were limited. Most couples would have known one another quite well for several years before getting married.

Courtship in Canada's rural areas was usually closely monitored. It was a process that began most often in church, at a social or a family celebration, and was subject to the rigours of Victorian respectability. Often a young man would have to ask the young woman or her parents for permission "to call" at a given time. Courting most often took place in the woman's parents' home, and in the initial stages would consist of a series of chaperoned visits. Later, perhaps, there would be the possibility of going walking, riding in a carriage, or sleighing together. In the mid-nineteenth century, formal love letters were often considered a romantic and normal part of the courtship process. There were books of instruction readily available advising young lovers on what to say, and if the process was still too difficult, it was possible to simply crib one's lines from the manual.

After a suitable period of time, the young man would invariably ask the woman's father for permission to marry his daughter. By the time of the Confederation era, arranged marriages were very much a thing of the past in Canada. Women certainly had to agree to a marriage, but nevertheless, the father of the bride normally reserved the right "to approve" a match. Parental approval was not just a one-way process; it was also

they were comfortable, their horizons were fairly narrow. Their culture and their situation offered few career alternatives to farming. Life on farms and in tiny villages a means of allowing an uncomfortable and stressed woman a reason to decline a suitor's proposal.

Weddings during most of the Confederation era were relatively simple affairs, with only the closest of friends and family attending. This was true especially in rural areas. Lavish and more extravagant celebrations would become customary closer to the turn of the century. Brides wearing white became fashionable only after Queen Victoria's wedding; and in Canada, the tradition only became commonplace in the late 1870s. Weddings were almost always held in the mornings, usually in a church, but sometimes in the bride's or groom's home. They would be followed by a small lunch or breakfast, with pieces of wedding cake and calling cards distributed as the guests left. The calling cards would advise guests as to when the newlyweds would be "at home" for visitors.

Given the restrictions in one's marriage and career possibilities, and the reasonably uniform socio-economic nature of Canadian rural society, marriage was as much a practical choice as it was a romantic one. And once married, there was little scope for making any changes to the customary roles people played within the family. Within the framework of rural society, traditional family roles were well-established, and well-accepted. All the evidence suggests that there was little impetus to change them. Although there were courageous pioneers, women's rights were not a prevalent issue. Men continued to be the breadwinners and women raised children and tended to domestic chores.

This was not a recipe for domestic misery, however. Canadian rural family life was based on practical but

A newlywed couple, posed in front of Niagara Falls, 1870s. They were ahead of their time. The concept of a honeymoon vacation would not become popular in Canada until the late 1890s.

affectionate relationships — but in the event that there was little or no affection, these relationships were also buttressed by the dictates of loyalty and economics. Divorce was not a viable option for most rural families, and the financial realities of farm life were such that there were no other alternatives to keeping families together as viable economic units.

Getting a divorce was nearly impossible in Ontario and Quebec, as these provinces didn't have divorce courts. If someone wanted a divorce, he or she had to make an appeal through Parliament, which was an option effectively open only to wealthy people who were willing to put up with the scrutiny and scorn that went with such an undertaking. The Maritimes had divorce courts, but the social and economic prohibitions against divorce were equally as strong there. And while it was possible to get a divorce in the United States, where the laws were considerably more liberal, American divorces only provided a limited degree of social respectability, as they had no legal standing in Canada. The courts in Canada made things even more difficult for the unhappily married. Adultery was the primary grounds for divorce during most of the Confederation era, and the courts frequently imposed a punitive element to any judgment, stipulating that the offending party could not remarry while their original spouse was alive.

In terms of the era's views on gender parity, it wasn't just a matter of attitude: women in the Confederation era were legally inferior to men. Women of the era had a long way to go. The BNA Act of 1867 used the word "persons" to refer to more than one person, and "he" when referring to one person. This wording was clarified in 1876, when a British judge ruled that "Women are persons in matters of pains and penalties, but are not persons in matters of rights and privileges."[1]

In virtually every aspect of their lives, women were repressed. An intrinsic part of that repressive culture was the period's legendarily puritanical and bizarre attitude to sex. An argument can be made that gender repression and Victorian neurotic sexual repression were two sides of the same coin, that Victorian anxieties about the future were in part bred in the changing economic and social structures of a newly industrialized society. They were obsessive and unsuccessful attempts to exert control over a society changing in ways its leaders neither understood nor wanted. While there may be some truth to this, it's also likely that gender roles were evolving logically and inevitably as society

A party of women enjoying a good laugh as they travel on the forward deck of a Lake Ontario steamboat, late 1860s.

industrialized and education levels rose, that the era's sexual concerns were rooted in ignorance of biology and human nature, as well as a poorly articulated desire to prevent women from achieving the same status as males, thereby preserving a manageable semblance of what the old society was like. In Canada, all of these elements were present in the Confederation decades. Canada displayed the same kinds of behaviours with regard to sex and the women's movement that surfaced in Britain and America.

Most men in the era were resistant to any change in the roles of the sexes and viewed the very notion of women's rights as politically preposterous; however, not all held that view. John A. Macdonald was the world's first democratic leader to attempt to give women the vote. In 1885, he introduced legislation on the subject, but it floundered in the House of Commons. Macdonald put the issue aside, but predicted that one day Canadian womanhood would "completely establish her equality as a human being and as a member of society with man."[2] He was decades ahead of his time, however, and his notions of a society where women would be equal was deemed so absurd it did not merit further serious legislative discussion for another decade. Instead, women's issues were temporarily subsumed by the labour and temperance movements and religious organizations.

Although women's rights movements were sneered at and generally treated with contempt, the women's movement grew slowly but steadily. Activists in the movement had to be cautious and secretive in their activities. For example, in Toronto, the women's rights movement had to operate under the innocuous title of "The Toronto Women's Literary Society."[3] It was a kind of camouflage that allowed women to leave home for the evening to discuss the issues of advancing women's rights.

There were, however, some gains made during the period and, although they were tentative, they were important. In several constituencies, women were granted property rights separate from their husbands. For example, the Public Lands of the Dominion Statute allowed homestead land to be given to a woman only if she was unmarried and had dependents under the age of majority. In Ontario, a law was passed in 1882 allowing unmarried women who held property to vote in municipal elections.

Very few were admitted to university programs, but during the later years of the period that began to change. Grace Anne Lockhart was the first woman to receive a baccalaureate in all of the British Empire when she graduated from New Brunswick's Mount

Allison College in 1875. In the same year, Jennie Trout was licensed in Toronto to practise medicine, but only after getting her medical degree from a woman's college in Pennsylvania.

Despite these exceptions, women were raised to believe that their place was in the home as a wife and mother. This expectation was true at all levels and in all ethnic groups. Only a small minority of bold and independent thinkers challenged the notion, and these were, for the most part, women whose circumstances gave them the opportunity to see beyond the confines of their situation.

In rural Canada, in particular, the role of a farmer's wife had evolved into a highly restrictive but economically indispensable function in society. Women on farms were raised and trained in the not inconsiderable tasks of running and managing a rural household. From dawn until dark, their lives involved an eclectic variety of diverse skills, such as cooking, animal husbandry, preserving foodstuffs, baking, cheese making, beekeeping, care of the sick and elderly, candle making, raising children, spinning wool, sewing clothing, butchering animals, gardening, cleaning, washing, and preparing scores of items that we buy today as manufactured goods. Like their husbands, who managed the never-ending list of chores outside the house, Confederation-era farm women were busy people.

Because Confederation-era farm women lived such frantically demanding lives, in hindsight it is easy to see that the women's movement was primarily an urban phenomenon. All the advances in women's rights during the period were made by women who lived in towns and cities. This might be explained, in part, because farm life was more of an equal partnership than urban life. But as important as the advances in this era were, they were limited, and the suffragette movement remained in its infancy.

One striking difference between rural Confederation-era families and modern ones was care of the elderly. Given the mortality statistics — women routinely outlived their husbands, often by considerable margins, it was quite normal for widows to move into the homes of their children. There was really no alternative to this arrangement. Life on a Canadian farm was a rigorous existence, where simple tasks, such as keeping the house warm in winter, entailed cutting wood and feeding a stove. They were chores that took energy and agility. In these circumstances, a single aging person on an isolated farm was usually unable to cope. In the event of dementia, there was not much that a family could do; children would normally be tasked with caring for the infirm, but often that task was too great for them. Elderly patients who became a hazard to themselves and their families and could not remain with the family were sometimes committed to poor houses or asylums in nearby towns. Such instances were exceptional, and occurred only if the option was available, which was not always the case. Those unfortunates who were sent to public institutions would end their days in harsh and appalling environments. Deprived of medical help and the affection of a family, they rarely survived long in their new surroundings.

Although the nuclear family was the predominant and most important social institution in the era, households often contained more than just family members.

As the size of farms grew, Confederation-era farmers often hired seasonal help. In the early years, these hired hands more often than not lived with the family, or on larger farms, such as on the Prairies at harvest time. They often lived in a bunk house next to the farm house, and many of them ate with the farmer's family.

As farms grew more prosperous, as most did throughout the Confederation decades, farm families had the means to take on additional help. Throughout the period it was not uncommon for them to have servants. In the early years of the century, 20 percent of rural servants were males, but by the 1840s, they were almost all young women. Domestic service was the most common employment for women in Canada, and we know from the 1891 census that Canada had over eighty-thousand such women working in private homes.[4]

Most farmers and their families regarded themselves as being ruggedly practical people, belonging to a large, relatively equal and independent society. It wasn't just nobility of spirit that underlay these attitudes. There was a practical basis for this impartiality; manpower was scarce, and people and talent had to be distributed how and when they found it. While they were not entirely innocent of class prejudices, most Canadian farmers regarded notions of restrictive class structures as belonging to the old country and urban status seekers. For them, there was little profit to be had devoting time or energy to developing a convoluted class system.[5]

On Canada's farms, young women employed as domestic help were not treated as social inferiors. In fact, from the statistical analyses of the period, we know that rural domestic servants were socially mobile and had a high turnover rate. By the early twentieth century, the field of domestic service in rural Canada had virtually ceased to exist — almost certainly because these women married into the local communities, or moved into the cities and towns as industrial work became available. Catharine Parr Traill painted a vivid picture of this mobility:

> What an inducement to young girls to emigrate is this! good wages, in a healthy and improving country; and what is better, in one where idleness and immorality are not the characteristics of the inhabitants: where steady industry is sure to be rewarded by marriage with young men who are able to place their wives in a very different station from that of servitude. How many young women who were formerly servants in my house, are now farmers' wives, going to church or the market towns with their own sleighs or light wagons, and in point of dress, better clothed than myself.[6]

Home children sent from Britain's poor houses also became a source of assistance on Confederation-era farms, and in many families these children were freely adopted and treated as new family members. On others, they were exploited and dealt with cruelly. Although the evidence for this latter category is entirely anecdotal, it is likely the number of children who were treated harshly was small.

What was beyond doubt regarding the employment and treatment of children was the prevalence of child labour during the Confederation era. Children did not have effective legal protection from being exploited as a source of labour in Canada until well into the twentieth century. Throughout the Confederation decades, working children were an important part of family life. In most towns and cities, the salaries made by children were essential for the economic survival of working-class families. In the same manner, Canadian farms could not get by without large numbers of children working.

Confederation-era Canadians regarded childhood much differently than we do today. For many, childhood was a much more abbreviated period of one's life. There was no conception of, or desire to understand, a child's mental or physical developmental periods. Children were given adult responsibilities years before they reached puberty. In the early years of the era, it was normal to have children as young as seven working as machine operators in textile mills in Montreal, as bellows operators in Nova Scotia's coal mines, as house and stable cleaners or stock boys in Toronto, or doing scores of tasks on farms across the country.

In 1861 Montreal, one-third of working-class boys under the age of fourteen were employed full-time. It probably was not much different in other cities. Nor did the situation improve throughout the Confederation decades. From the 1870s to the 1890s, the percentage of child labourers rose steadily.[7] In 1884 in Ontario, the Factories Act was introduced, which established the working age as twelve years old for boys and fourteen years old for girls. For both groups, it restricted the hours of work to ten hours a day, or sixty hours a week — with clauses nullifying the Act in the event of undefined "breakdowns" or "exigencies of the trade." It was better than nothing, but not much. There were no enforcement mechanisms in the bill and verification procedures were never defined or implemented. The ages cited in the Factory Act are worth noting. Twelve-year-old boys and fourteen-year-old girls were, for the purposes of full employment, considered adults. It wasn't unusual for the time. The concept of adolescence did not exist until the early 1900s, when American psychologists began to conduct a scientific analysis of the transition to adulthood.

As a practice, most Canadians regarded child labour as being essential to a healthy economy. This kind of thinking was so accepted that when several bills to prohibit child labour were introduced in Parliament in the 1870s and early 1880s, they were all soundly defeated, or simply allowed to languish on the order paper without ever being debated.

In New Brunswick, a typical rural schoolhouse of the Confederation decades with teacher and students. Although the school year was short, free schooling meant that overall literacy levels in Canada were high compared to the rest of the world.

Educators in the nation's school system were not opposed to child labour. Schooling was intentionally designed to give working-class children and farm children access to free, compulsory education; but, along with this, the school year was designed specifically to enable children to spend most of the year in full employment. Ontario was a good example. The Ontario School Act of 1879 was written so that each municipality was obliged to provide children between the ages of seven and twelve only four months of schooling each year.[8] The remaining eight months were not reserved for holidays, but to allow children the chance to do farm and factory work.

The education system was also designed to ensure that women received a minimal level of instruction. With the rise of compulsory education in Canada in the early 1870s, the number of girls in the system almost equalled the number of boys.[9] However, the prevalent social expectations were such that girls were encouraged to leave school by no later than fourteen. Beyond this, education for girls was usually only provided at private colleges, and for those who could afford it. The colleges generally made no attempt to meet any clearly defined academic standards; instead, they trained middle-class students in the social graces and prepared a growing number to become school teachers. Teaching was one of the few professions open to women. Because the period mindset was that women had special "nurturing" aptitudes, women were accepted as teachers; and, perhaps more importantly, for governments anxious to keep rising education costs in check, they could be hired at much lower wages than men.

Aboriginal schooling in the period reflected the indifferent and brutally offhand government approach to the treatment of First Nations. In the early colonial years of the Confederation decades, a number of voluntary "manual schools" were established for aboriginal children, largely with the intent of assimilating them by teaching them to become farmers. For reasons already discussed, these efforts failed right across the country. With the Indian Act, the federal government assumed responsibility for the education of all Status Indians. Manual schools were followed by a further feeble attempt to create local day schools, which were run almost entirely by missionaries. There were serious problems with these schools. They were characterized by underfunding, insensitivity to languages of instruction, cultural disdain, inappropriate curriculum, inadequate teaching, and, not surprisingly, poor attendance.

In 1879, Canada, in imitation of a U.S. model, adopted a system of residential schools. To save money, wherever possible existing mission schools were used. Attendance eventually became compulsory. To achieve this, primary-school-age aboriginal children were forcibly wrenched from their families and sent off for years to be schooled in either English or French. While some schools were reasonably well-run, many others were not. Many residential schools had virtually no supervision, and many of them experienced all the problems of the previous system, but they were run with an institutional harshness and a malignance that is now difficult to comprehend.

In virtually all schools, small children were torn from their families and moved hundreds of miles away.

A school for aboriginal children, northern Manitoba, early 1880s.

In the worst schools, small children were physically punished for speaking their own language; their ration scale in many cases was criminally inadequate; they were routinely housed in inadequately heated barrack-style accommodation; and many were subject to physical and sexual abuse from their teachers and older children. Over three thousand children died from tuberculosis, and the standard of education was such that few progressed beyond the most basic levels. When they completed their schooling, they were inadequately prepared to compete for jobs in the larger economy.

The system lasted in one form or another for almost a century. Starting in the Confederation decades, several generations of aboriginal children were kept out of sight, living unpublicized for decades in horrendous conditions, with widespread disease, and a mortality rate similar to a low-intensity war. Residential schools inflicted massive psychological damage on generations of vulnerable children. It is an ugly part of our history that the rest of Canada is only gradually beginning to accept.

* * *

While most Victorian Canadians had an education system that was inferior in virtually every way to today's, those who lived in rural areas had a diet that was substantially superior. Confederation-era Canadians suffered from diseases that have been largely eradicated; their water was often unfit to drink; they had no antibiotics; their occupational safety standards were far below current ones; and their overall mortality rate was higher, but for the majority of the population, especially those who lived in the rural areas, their basic diet was healthier. They rarely ate processed food of any sort, and their consumption of sugar and salt (despite preserving their meat in brine) was well below ours. Victorian Canadians generally ate fresh food. Confederation-era diets were high in regionally grown fruits, locally raised vegetables, and whole grains. And while they had nothing like the variety of choice to be found in a Canadian supermarket today, the food they did eat was basic, nutritious, and free from pesticides and drugs.

Processed foods would start to be introduced in quantity to the Canadian diet near the turn of the century, with the introduction of sugar-sweetened condensed milk and canned fruits swimming in syrup. However, for Canadians of the Confederation era, their diet consisted in the main of numerous kinds of root vegetables, legumes, seasonal vegetables, corn, whole grain breads, apples, pears, plums, pumpkins, berries, pork, beef, poultry, and fish.

Given the physically intensive nature of their work and daily lives, most rural Canadians and urban labourers of the period consumed far more calories than we do.[10] Despite that, as a society, they did not experience the problems with obesity that we now have.

There was never an issue with the amount of food being produced in the country, but there were problems associated with the diets of many in the Confederation era. Social and economic inequities meant that elements of society periodically went hungry and were malnourished. There were also other dietary problems that cut across all class and regional lines. For example, we know that alcohol consumption was very high and caused widespread health, economic, and social problems. Our understanding as to the exact scale of this problem is speculative, as records are almost all anecdotal, but we are certain that high alcohol consumption had a harmful effect on society. We know from production and sales statistics that drinking habits in Canada changed during the Confederation decades. In the early years of the century, cider and beer, which were often home brewed, were the most common drinks; but starting in the middle of the century, spirit consumption rose swiftly. Domestic whisky and Jamaican rum sales increased on a year-over-year basis.

Not surprisingly, at the same time, temperance movements gained traction in every part of Canada.[11] The temperance movement had its initial roots in immigrant British and American evangelical Baptists and Methodists, but the cause also had strong support from urban middle-class businessmen, who wanted sober, reliable employees. Although the Canada Temperance Act in 1878 granted regions the power to implement prohibition at local levels, national prohibition was never actually implemented during the Confederation decades. However, failure to implement national prohibition during the Confederation decades did not deter

An Ontario farmer harvests a substantial turnip crop, 1870s. The introduction of fertilizers, crop rotation, and factory-made agricultural machinery in the Confederation era increased yields and meant that food was plentiful.

the federal government from imposing prohibition on First Nations. From the time of the Royal Proclamation, Canada had created a series of laws outlawing the sale of liquor to First Nations, laws which eventually were repealed in the Indian Act of 1876 and were not substantially changed to give local band councils the authority to decide for themselves how to deal with the issue until 1985.[12] New Brunswickers, on the other hand, voted in favour of prohibition in 1852, but the law was only implemented within certain counties, and it had several loopholes that allowed anyone who wanted to drink to get around the restriction. Similarly, by 1850, over half of Quebec's francophones, influenced by a group of charismatic priests, had taken temperance pledges, but the provincial legislators never took any action to implement prohibition.[13] The temperance movement exerted a strong undercurrent in nineteenth-century Canada, but actual prohibition only surfaced regionally for short periods in the early twentieth century.

Funerals and the attitudes toward death during the Confederation era were markedly different than modern sensibilities. One of the most striking differences was that fewer people died in hospitals. The most common causes of death throughout the era were from infectious diseases. If you were terminally ill and were in a hospital, you would usually be sent home to die amongst family and friends. Hospitals were reserved for those likely to recover.

The result of this was that death was something much closer, more immediate, and more familiar to Confederation-era Canadians. They experienced it first-hand, in their bedrooms and in their parlours. Seriously ill people who were dying at home would sometimes have their bed set up in the parlour. Downstairs was usually closer to a stove and therefore warmer during the cold months, and the family could more readily attend to a patient. Often, the family and close friends would remain at the patient's bedside day and night, waiting for death, anxious to hear their loved one's last words.

After death, the dead were often kept within the home. Family members washed and dressed the body. The practice of embalming bodies was rare during the Confederation period. Embalming has its origins with the ancient Egyptians, but it did not become popular in North America until after Abraham Lincoln's death, when his body was preserved for an elaborate state funeral. In Canada, the practice did not begin to become popular until the early 1900s.

A local carpenter would usually make and deliver a simple coffin to the bereaved family. The coffin would be taken to a church in a wagon, often by horses draped in black cloth and decorated with black ostrich feathers. Later in the period, in towns and cities, livery stables would rent the use of a black, glass-sided hearse. Funeral parlours, which evolved into funeral homes in the twentieth century, did not begin to come into vogue in Canada until late in the 1880s. It wasn't until the 1920s that customs changed and care of the dead was routinely outsourced to undertakers. As funerals became more elaborate and removed from the home, and death became less familiar, the undertaker evolved into a funeral director, who handled all aspects of a funeral, except the actual religious ceremonies. Funerals were invariably held in the mornings, and in the more genteel classes, personal invitations were sent out requesting attendance. Mourners would dress in black and accompany the coffin from the church to the gravesite. In winter, coffins would be stored in a stone or brick mausoleum until the ground thawed sufficiently to allow internment to take place. Even for the poorest in Canada, proper burial came with a coffin, a church service, a plot, a headstone, and a decent wake. To be buried with anything less was considered a disgrace, and even the poorest Canadians scrimped and saved. The poorest put money aside in burial clubs and friendly societies to ensure that in death they avoided shame and were given a proper "send off."[14]

Once a death occurred, families would open their windows, close the blinds and drapes, and cover all mirrors. This tradition had its origins in superstitions related to the passage of spirits and bad luck, but in the Confederation era the practice grew into a traditional custom. Frequently, as a sign of respect, clocks would be stopped at the hour of death. Front doors would be draped with cloth to warn others that someone had died within. Black cloth was used to signify the death of an adult and white cloth to mark the death of an infant or child.

Confederation-era Canadians had very specific rules regarding mourning clothes. It was considered to be bad manners to wear any colourful clothing to a funeral, and the bereaved were expected to wear mourning clothes, usually black, for a year or more while they were in "deep mourning." For at least another six months, while they were in "half mourning," they would wear some conspicuous piece of black clothing to indicate that they were still observing a period of grief.

Perhaps one of the most remarkable practices that developed during the period was photographing the dead. If the family did not have a photograph of the deceased, which was most often a child who had died suddenly, a photographer would take a picture of the dressed corpse. Sometimes the corpse was braced up in a sitting position surrounded by his or her relatives, and not infrequently the eyes were propped open to feign life, but most often the departed would be resting in a natural sleeping position. To twenty-first-century

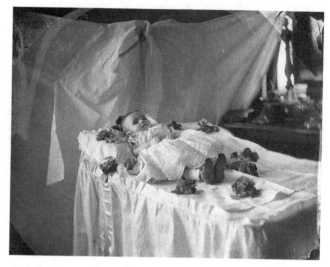

An infant corpse photographed at her wake, Montreal, 1869.

sensibilities, this seems macabre, but for people who were accustomed to death and handling corpses, they obviously thought the practice was appropriate, as it provided a grieving family some means of remembering a loved one.

Chapter Sixteen

ATTITUDES AND BELIEFS

Canada was an overwhelmingly Christian country, with a handful of major denominations. Without the aboriginal peoples, Canada in 1871 was 98 percent Christian. Roman Catholics, who were primarily of French, Irish, and Scottish descent, made up 41 percent of the population, while a further 57 percent were divided amongst various Protestant groups. During the Confederation decades, the Anglicans started as the most numerous group but over the years lost considerable ground to the Presbyterians, Methodists, Baptists, Lutherans, and numerous Evangelical sects.[1]

Christian churches in the period were influential, energetic, and powerful forces within their respective communities. Church attendance was high, and church-centred life was extremely popular in both English and French Canada. Churches assumed not only religious importance, but they also ran many of the public charities, and, in both urban and rural areas, were at the centre of much of the social life.

Few Canadians during this period identified themselves as being agnostic or having no religious affiliation. This stands in fairly sharp contrast to the UK and America's northern states, where, especially in the later years of the era, there was a new embryonic and public sense of religious uncertainty. Victorian angst about religion was largely based on recent challenges to conventional religious tenets and literal interpretations of the Bible arising from Charles Darwin's findings on evolution, as well as discoveries, by several geologists, of the earth's geological age. Canadians were a literate population, and they were likely as aware of these new scientific discoveries as Britons or Americans. Canada's absence of religious anguish may reflect, not a shallow lack of moral inquiry, but a habit of not challenging the status quo. This trait likely had its roots in how the two major cultures co-existed. Both French and English understood the art of getting along in a time of relative religious antagonism. From a political perspective, Canada was not yet two solitudes, but had over the years developed into a kind of easy social, political, and economic symbiosis. People had adopted a "live and let live" attitude when it came to core beliefs that were not creating conflict with one another. In this manner, they were likely to refrain from disrupting things, and self-identified with the cultural features of their religious affiliation, regardless of their private beliefs.

For a time during the mid- and late nineteenth century, belief in spiritualism was also popular. Although it was much more in vogue in America and Britain, it did have a short currency in southern Ontario and Montreal from the 1850s through to the 1870s. Séances and the idea of communicating with the dead became popular around the same time as extensive use of the telegraph. There was also considerable interest in the new field of mesmerism, which proposed to bring about medical cures by regulating the flows of animal magnetism in a human body and aligning these magnetic flows with universal magnetic fields. These beliefs were popular only briefly and their appeal was likely consistent with a heightened interest in science and a general fascination with the era's advances in knowledge.

Apart from religious beliefs, Confederation-era Canadians shared a number of overarching attitudes that distinguished them from other countries. Canada was a relatively peaceful and orderly nation because of its geography, its colonial parentage, and good luck. But there was a fourth element to its good fortune, and that was that Canadians trusted in the rule of law. Canadian conflicts had all been small ones. The rebellions of 1837 and 1838, the Red River Rebellion, and even the post-Confederation-era North-West Rebellion, while indicating larger social problems, were all fairly mild by comparison with the violence that wracked other countries during the period. Problems were generally dealt with, not always successfully, but within democratic structures.

Where Canadians were similar to the British and the Americans was in a number of nineteenth-century attitudes. Chief amongst these was the overriding belief in respectability. Victorian respectability had numerous facets. It most obviously displayed itself as a belief in manners. The period had rules that governed almost all aspects of life. There was an accepted and "proper" way of doing things for every conceivable situation. Propriety became a mark of distinction, a sure sign that one knew how to behave, and was comfortably a part of a decent class of society. As a result, people deported themselves in a stiff and dignified manner. This in turn led to a kind of conformity that successive generations would find constricting and artificial. Examples of this can be found in things like prudishness. Victorians were neurotically unwilling to discuss or mention subjects that lay on the margins of good taste. Discussions of things such as sex and sexuality were socially prohibited as they violated respectability. Canadians were by no means immune from this trait. This desire for respectability and propriety led to a serious and sober kind of conformity. Even the language was, by today's standards, somewhat pompous, mannered, and pretentious. But this obsession for respectability was almost certainly driven by an underlying purpose.

With the Industrial Revolution, class divisions changed. The middle class grew in terms of its size and influence; and with the growth of the middle class came a kind of social anxiety, which had at its heart the recently affluent middle classes' desire for social acceptance. In this new order, people were defined by their jobs and their station in life rather than their family backgrounds. Showing that one knew how to behave, how to speak, and how to conduct oneself was implicit proof that one had arrived. Being in the middle class was incredibly important in a culture where the great majority of the population were descendants of those who had spent the last several millennia at the bottom of the social pyramid.

These factors were at play in Canada as well, but there were other influences changing the equation. The middle class in Canada differed substantially from both the middle class in the UK and the newly industrialized cities of the northern states.* Canada's middle class was overwhelmingly rural, while in these other regions, the middle class was growing as a result of booming urban markets for professional, trade, and commercial services. Because the majority of Canada's middle class was

made up of proud and relatively self-sufficient frontier farmers, the middle class was initially not as well-to-do. This in turn meant that entrance to the middle class was much more open, and its values were shared by a larger proportion of people. While Britain and America's booming northern cities were developing socially in the shape of a pyramid, Canada was growing more in the shape of a milk bottle.

Canadians, like their British and American counterparts, believed that work was a duty, that it was character building and good for one's soul. The Protestant ethic of industry thrift and hard work had by the 1840s drifted across denominational boundaries. By the mid-nineteenth century, it had become thoroughly ingrained in middle-class thinking. The Irish dairy farmer, no less than the Anglican shop owner in the next village, regarded "undeserving poor" as those who were poor through no fault of their own and could not work. This category included widows and orphans, the very elderly, and the disabled. It did not include the "deserving poor," those who were capable of working but did not. The deserving poor included those who were victims of any of the larger economic changes that threw thousands out of work, as well as those who were considered to be in any way morally suspect, such as vagrants or unwed mothers.

In this there was a strange contradiction. In Canada, like the rest of the new world, the middle class accepted people into its ranks fairly readily, probably because most Canadians were within a generation or two of being poor themselves: Scottish crofters who had their cottages torn down, starving Irish, families fleeing English workhouses, and the sons of American

---

* The rural middle class in America's northern states shared some similar class characteristics with Canada. However, rural society in the northern states was generally older and more established. In the 1840–60 period, the most dynamic and influential elements in American society were in its large rapidly industrializing cities, a phenomenon which would not appear in Canada until the early twentieth century.

farmers seeking new land all shared this acceptance into a large amorphous middle class. As willing as they were to regard these new immigrants as equals, they also readily accepted the era's prevailing judgment as to what constituted deserving poverty. What differentiated Canada from the industrial cities of England was that Canada could much more readily absorb large numbers of the poor, and there were relatively fewer poor unemployed people in Canada. There were futures to be had homesteading, jobs to be had in the lumber industry or as a hired hand on a farm. Canadians did not have to deal with masses of unemployable workers drifting into England's cities. In Canada, the percentage of impoverished people was much smaller and therefore more manageable. In this manner, constant low-level economic growth and steady demographic growth did much to shape the national character.

Along with Confederation era's middleclass values of respectability and the dignity of work went the concept of integrity. Integrity was laden with class overtones.

First- and second-generation Scottish Canadians, Eastern Ontario, 1882. The middle classes in the Confederation decades were not only comfortable; they enjoyed a standard of living and security that would have astonished their grandparents' generation.

In the early years of the period, being a gentleman, or a lady, meant one belonged to the aristocracy, but during the Confederation decades, being a gentleman morphed into meaning that one subscribed to a certain lofty moral code. The gentleman was idealized as being a man of unassailable integrity, a kind of modern day, saintly Arthurian prince.[2] It was an aspiration rather than a reality. That image of class integrity was contradicted by obvious inconsistencies. The era's outward appearance of restraint, dignity, and righteousness contrasted with the pervasiveness of the era's commercial exploitation, widespread prostitution, child labour, and utter disinterest in the welfare of dispossessed classes, such as the urban poor and First Nations. And while it is dangerous to pretend to be outraged about the shortcomings of previous generations, it is fair to say that this was a generation that prided itself on its sense of integrity, rectitude, and morality. However, Victorian Canadians were no more or less virtuous than any other generation, and had their own strengths and failings.

One issue from the Confederation era that surfaces periodically is the subject of racism. It is a reasonable concern. Canadian society of the period was racist. Many of the English-speaking peoples in Canada believed that the British Empire was leading the world into a new and better age. English-speaking Canadians believed as a matter of course that the English race was demonstrably superior to all others. British North Americans, along with their fellow members of the Empire in Britain, were utterly convinced of the innate superiority of the British over the inhabitants of other countries. This was simply assumed as a matter of common knowledge.

Most Victorian thinkers of the time did not hesitate to question this. Charles Kingsley, the famous social reformer and a prominent Anglican priest, summed up the prevailing spirit of the time as Britain's "glorious work which God seems to have laid on the English race, to replenish the earth and subdue it."[3]

The best that can be said is that it was a time of massive contradictions. Closer to home, George Brown, the founder of *The Globe* newspaper, was forever regaling his readers to be wary of the dangers posed by Catholics, Jews, and Irish; yet at the same time, he was a passionate abolitionist and a strong proponent of the integration of escaped black American slaves and white Canadians. Canadians were generally ardent supporters of the Underground Railroad, but at the same time, few would tolerate racially mixed schools or hotels. People's perspectives were limited, confused, and evolving.

Racism was not just a British failing. In the nineteenth century, it was a global problem. National, ethnic, and religious chauvinism (the word would not be used in its current meaning until 1945) was an intrinsic component of every culture. Notions of racial tolerance and understanding had existed for thousands of years, yet these beliefs only assumed their widespread and current emphasis after the world had endured two catastrophic world wars. A hundred years before, racist views were common. What kept Canada moving forward and prevented the country from sinking into a nasty squalid autocracy were its democratic traditions and adherence to the rule of law.

The rule of law and the justice system in the Confederation era displayed some noteworthy differences and similarities to what we know today. Although crimes of the period were comparable to modern offences, many laws, the courts, the police, and the penal system were very different. The Confederation era was a period that saw the abandonment of public executions, the rise of modern police forces, and growing social advocacy for juveniles, victims, and criminals, but in many respects, it was a much more lawless time than the present.

One of the most notable differences in nineteenth-century crime was the frequency of riots. Before Canada had trained and disciplined professional police forces, demonstrations and altercations quickly escalated, often turning into prolonged mob violence. Almost always, the fighting had religious or political associations. Some of the most significant Confederation-era riots were: the Irish sectarian Battle of York Point in Saint John, New Brunswick, in 1845; the burning of the Montreal parliament buildings in 1849 after the Rebellion Losses Bill; the Gavazzi riots in Quebec City and Montreal in 1853, which were triggered by anti-clerical lectures given by an Italian ex-monk; and the Jubilee Riots in Toronto in 1875, which was just one of that city's many bloody outbreaks of violence between Catholics and Protestant Orangemen. Toronto alone had an estimated twenty-six riots between 1839 and 1860, almost all of them sectarian in nature. New Brunswick listed eighteen similar riots that had to be quelled by troops during the same period.[4] Many of these riots involved fatalities, either from shootings by rioters or troops having to fire into the crowds to disperse the mob. Even with the advent of police forces, things didn't initially get much better. In Toronto for example, members of the police

force who had been recruited from the city's Orange Lodges often actively joined in the rioting.[5]

Before the creation of municipal police forces, larger towns and cities, such as Halifax, Montreal, and Quebec, hired armed, untrained constables to assist watchmen. In the event of mob violence, the British Army and local militia units were called out to restore order.[6]

By the 1830s, municipalities recognized the need for specialized policing. Toronto raised the first real permanent police force in 1834, and other cities followed soon after. In rural townships and villages, judges and justices of the peace conscripted local men for short periods of time to serve as untrained constables and supervisory "high constables." These rural constables served warrants, escorted prisoners, and attended court, but there was nothing in their duties in terms of responsive or proactive policing. In those early years, police also carried out numerous functions that are now conducted by other civil organizations. In the Confederation decades, police served as health and fire inspectors, checked on tavern and hotel licenses, as well as enforced regulations relating to agricultural produce and animal control.

It is difficult to assess the actual crime rates during the period, as intensive policing was confined to cities with permanent police forces, and the bulk of the population lived in the country. In the rural areas, it is likely that, given the absence of police, the distances, the relative isolation of most of the population, and poor communications, many crimes went unreported. As well as this, the actual court proceedings were not recorded for most of the period. Existing documents indicate that while there was serious crime, the overwhelming majority of criminal behaviour consisted of public drunkenness, vandalism, brawling, petty theft, prostitution and other undefined acts of immorality, the breaking of local ordinances, the abandonment of indentured service contracts, and swearing.[7] We do know that juveniles were treated as adults for most of the period. From 1846 to 1857, three hundred juveniles were imprisoned with adults in New Brunswick alone.[8]

In the earliest years of the period, children were give horrific prison sentences. Whippings were common, and children were locked up in the same cells as hardened criminals and the mentally ill. One ten-year-old boy was incarcerated for seven years in the Kingston Penitentiary. Within his first eight months he was flogged fifty-seven times for misdemeanours, which included the crimes of laughing and staring.[9] Juvenile "industrial homes" were opened in the late 1850s, but throughout the decades, physical punishment of minors was considered to be the most effective and economical means of handling delinquents. Those advocating more lenient treatment of children in the justice system were not successful in seeing major reforms until the adoption of the new Criminal Code in 1892.[10]

The period between being arrested and the time the accused was tried was very short. Minor offenses came to trial within days and trials for major offenses were underway within a month. Trials for serious crimes rarely lasted more than a few days, as there were strict limits on who could be called as an expert witness. Juries were often eliminated, and up to half of the trials for serious crimes saw defendants waive their rights to trial by jury. Courts of Error and Appeal were instituted in Canada in 1849, which was decades earlier than they were in Britain. The process was completely uncoupled from the trial courts with the establishment of a separate appeals court in 1876.[11]

The Confederation decades had their share of famous crimes. The most notorious one of the period was the Cypress Hills Massacre in 1873, when twenty-three men, women, and children of the Assiniboine First Nation were killed. It took two-and-a-half months for word of this atrocity to get back to Ottawa, but the news hastened the raising of the North-West Mounted Police who were sent out to bring stability to the Prairies. The case dragged on for almost a decade and, although years later three arrests were eventually made, no one was ever successfully prosecuted.

The next most famous crime of the Confederation era was the mob killing of the "Black Donnellys" near London, Ontario. The Donnellys were an Irish immigrant family, well-known as unsavoury, small-time criminals and violent bullies. In the middle of a snow storm, one night in February 1880, a mob attacked and burned two of their houses, murdering five people, including children. Despite the eyewitness testimony of a surviving child, no one was ever charged with or convicted of the crimes.

Chapter Seventeen

INSTITUTIONAL LIFE

Government institutions during the Confederation Era were relatively austere by present standards. The BNA Act gave the federal government responsibility for the regulation of most matters of trade and commerce, criminal law, and for those issues where the legal or practical jurisdiction spanned more than one province. In turn, the provinces received control of "generally all matters of a merely local or private nature in the Province."[1]

From the outset, Canada and the provinces had substantial and well-established bureaucracies to run their organizations.* In the 1860s, Canada carefully followed the very recent British example of developing a civil service that was proficient, professional, and selected for their jobs on the basis of competence via an impartial selection process.[2] The men who established Canada's public service were on the whole successful. Canada was fortunate in having a lean and efficient public service with traditions of competence and professional integrity.

Over the years, the administrative, regulatory, and financial arms of government and civil society have assumed greater responsibilities and grown much larger. We are accustomed to thinking of national bureaucracies as being faceless and colourless, and while this may be true for some, the era's hospitals, prisons, charitable institutions, and military provide a fascinating and revealing glimpse of the era's character.

Canadian hospitals and medical care evolved substantially during the Confederation decades. In the 1840s, most acute and chronic medical care was carried

---

* By way of comparison, in terms of the public service's relative size, complexity, importance, and breadth of responsibility, while Canada's population is now ten times larger than it was at the time of Confederation, the national public service is 271 times larger.

out in the home. There were few hospitals, and the ones that existed were small and located only in larger towns and cities. There was also, up until the very early 1860s, a social stigma associated with being admitted to hospital. Those who could afford it hired doctors to look after them at home. Hospitals were seen as a kind of charity, a place for treatment of the needy. Being admitted to a hospital meant accepting a loss of control over one's life by allowing your treatment to be directed entirely by strangers.

Fear of hospitals was not entirely unfounded. During the Confederation era there was little understanding of germ theory. Although in the late 1850s, Pasteur had discovered the nature of germs and their relation to disease, his ideas took a long time before they were accepted by the medical community. By the 1880s, many doctors still believed in "miasma," a theory of infections based on foul airs. As a result, hospitals throughout the Confederation era had high rates of post-operative infections. Operations themselves were also rudimentary procedures. Because of the risk of infection, amputations were common and wounds and bleeding were cauterized with hot irons or boiling oil. Ether's use as an anesthetic began in Canada in the late 1840s and was eventually replaced by chloroform, both of which had serious and often life-threatening after-effects.*

Another reason people tended to avoid hospitals was in part due to the roaring trade in quack medicines. Dubious remedies abounded for practically every

ailment. Liniments, pills, oils, tonics, and pastes were sold to treat every known illness. There was no effective legal regulation of medicines in Canada until the introduction of the Proprietary or Patent Medicine Act in 1909. Before then, the ill, the gullible and the desperate bought fraudulent remedies in large quantities. Pharmacies existed, and they were regulated as early as 1867, but during the period, the pharmacist's role was primarily making and preparing drugs rather than regulating their sale and distribution.

One home medicine that was readily available without prescription was laudanum, sometimes called tincture of opium. A morphine derivative, its use was widespread throughout the Confederation era. In the absence of other medications, such as aspirin, people self-medicated with laudanum for every conceivable ailment. However, the most common conditions the drug was used for were asthma, diarrhea, headache, toothache, and arthritis. As a result, people regularly became addicted to laudanum, yet surprisingly, after the late eighteenth century, there was little evidence of laudanum's use as a recreational drug. In the same tradition of home-based remedies, cocaine eventually became popular as a medicinal product in a number of treatments, but its use did not become commonplace in Canada until after the Confederation era.

Throughout the Confederation decades, dental work in Canada was rudimentary. There were few qualified dentists in the country, and for most of the period, those who were qualified were trained via a four- or six-month apprenticeship. The resultant skill levels from this haphazard form of qualification varied from amateurish to

---

* One of the first people to use chloroform as an anaesthetic during the period was Abraham Lincoln, who in 1862 insisted it be used on him during a tooth extraction.

dangerous. Many dental apprentices went on to became itinerant dentists who visited remote communities on a periodic basis.

Because there were so few dentists, most dental work during the period was performed by local physicians, who also had minimal training in dentistry. As a result, dental work throughout the period was often appallingly crude. Pulling teeth was the most common treatment for virtually all ailments. It was a painful and unsophisticated procedure, which more often than not entailed infection and damage to the patient's jaw bone. Anaesthetics were rarely used. Instead, the common practice was to "freeze" the affected area by holding ice against it prior to extracting the tooth. This only provided slight relief from pain. Very wealthy Canadians could get porcelain teeth made in Toronto and Montreal, but most often, the more affluent had their false teeth and rudimentary fillings made from gold and silver. Things began to improve near the end of the period. The first dental college was established in Toronto in 1875, but it would not be until well into the twentieth century that there were sufficient numbers of dentists to meet the country's needs.

It would be wrong to think of the Confederation period as being forty years of home-based medical incompetence. Although the era did not have anything like the modern emphasis on research and development, Canada did have its own teaching hospitals. The first true Canadian teaching hospital was the Montreal General Hospital, which started training doctors in the late 1820s. Canadian teaching hospitals were not just imitations of European or American institutions. They

were innovative in their medical teaching practices. For example, Montreal General pioneered the art of bedside teaching, while Dartmouth's Nova Scotia Hospital was one of the first hospitals anywhere to teach and develop the field of occupational therapy.

Canada was much slower in training nurses. The first nursing schools did not open until 1881 at Toronto's General Hospital. Five years later, Montreal's Women's Hospital graduated its first nursing class. Educating nurses in the medical arts was a radical departure from the past. Few nurses, both lay or religious, had any medical training before the 1880s. Their primary functions were to watch over their patients and keep them clean. In Canada's lay hospitals there was also a distinct social hierarchy amongst the nursing staff, as middle-class women were hired in a supervisory role to monitor both the nursing staff and the maids who did the laundry and cleaning.

General hospitals were originally secular hospitals, as opposed to hospitals run by religious orders, most of which were run by nuns who had taken vows of poverty. Despite this, throughout the Confederation era, all hospitals ran on a precarious basis. They operated on public donations, government grants, and whatever they could get by way of patient fees. Often there wasn't enough money. In 1867 for example, the Toronto General hospital had to close for a year due to a lack of funding.

Mental illness was never well understood by the medical community during the Confederation era. However, a small number of doctors realized that the mentally ill could be treated better than they were. The early nineteenth century was a time when those

Two of the first of Canada's professionally trained nurses, Ontario, late nineteenth century.

unless the condition healed on its own, few psychiatric patients of the period ever improved.[3]

By 1857, "lunatic asylums" had been established in Newfoundland, Nova Scotia, Prince Edward Island, New Brunswick, Quebec, and Ontario. The asylums of the Confederation era were in reality little better than prisons. Lunatic asylums served as warehouses for the mentally ill: the food was appalling, communicable diseases were rife, individual care was haphazard and, more often than not, non-existent. The provincial asylums were regarded as institutions of last resort for those with prolonged and untreatable illnesses, or who could no longer be cared for by their families. For those mentally ill individuals who were arrested for vagrancy or more serious crimes, judges and juries could acquit a defendant on grounds of insanity. Special accommodation in prisons was made for the criminally insane, but in practice what the inmates received was little more than solitary confinement in a nine foot by five foot cell.[4]

A revealing indication of the official perspective on asylums and prisons can be seen in how they were grouped for government administrative purposes. Throughout the 1850s and '60s, the oversight body in Ontario consisted of a "Board of Inspectors of Prisons, Asylums, and Public Charities."[5] It was consistent with a world view that made little practical distinction between criminality, poverty, mental disability, unemployment, and alcoholism.

In line with this way of thinking, the state of prisons and jails in the Confederation era revealed much about the character of the society. Prior to the Confederation era, judicial punishment included a range of sentences,

suffering from mental illness were simply housed in jails and prisons. Although this practice wasn't entirely eliminated in the period, there was a movement to try to understand mental illness and deal with it more humanely. Unfortunately, the approach that was adopted was to treat the problem as a moral failing, and such as: the death penalty, flogging, mutilation, branding, and exile. John Howard, an influential British advocate of penal reform in the late eighteenth century, lobbied for a number of changes. He believed that the judicial system should focus on reform and deterrence rather than vengeance. Howard believed that criminality was caused by a lack of properly instilled moral values and structure in one's life. He urged such things as separating prisoners in cells in accordance with the degree of their crimes, providing intensive religious training, employing convicts at hard labour, enforcing prohibitions against the sale of liquor to prisoners, and providing prisoners with adequate clothing.[6] Howard's ideas gained currency in North America, and eventually found their way into the Canadian penal system via American examples. One of the results was the establishment of the Kingston Penitentiary in 1835.

The Kingston Penitentiary was Canada's largest non-military building of its time. An imposing structure, it housed 880 prisoners in cells, with each original cell measuring six feet by two feet. Prisoners were kept in absolute silence, except for when they were allowed to speak in the course of their duties. Prisoners worked on a central shop floor manufacturing leather goods and woodwork, cutting stone, and metalsmithing on a forge. Women performed compulsory needlework. Their finished goods were sold by bid on commercial markets.

Few Canadians of the period showed any interest in prisons, and this in turn resulted in little supervision of their management. Prisoners in penitentiaries were required to live in what was called partial isolation. They were forbidden to speak to one another in order to better reflect upon their wrongdoings. Food was execrable. Floggings could be handed out on the recommendation of a guard, and chaining prisoners in their cells was common. Troublesome prisoners were placed for days on end into the "box," a wooden, coffin-like case with a small breathing hole. Local jails were little better. In 1861, an observer of the Ottawa Jail found that the cells were damp and dingy, women, children and men were routinely held in the same rooms, and toilets were dark, unwholesome, and "overflowing with abomination."[7]

Charitable institutions in the Confederation era showed a similar improvement from the period that preceded them. For example, as we've seen, the homeless and the destitute were popularly and officially divided into classes of the deserving and undeserving poor. Despite this categorization, the poor were generally regarded with suspicion, as there was a popular, deep-rooted notion that giving the poor charity would encourage "idleness."

New Brunswick provides a good example as to how attitudes to charity changed. In the early years of the nineteenth century, the city of Saint John had scores of paupers. It was a port, and people often arrived sick, orphaned, or otherwise incapable of working. The colony had, in the eighteenth century, instituted laws that tasked parishes with responsibility for the poor. These early laws were based upon English precedent — a precedent that was established in the Elizabethan era. Because the poor tended to congregate in the urban areas, the residents of Saint John felt that the laws placed an undue burden on them. To help defray their expenses, they held auctions and gave the lowest bidders money to house the poor as they best saw fit. When that proved to be inadequate, a tax was levied on dog owners to help pay for the upkeep of paupers. The dog tax proved to be insufficient, and the funding source was broadened to include fines levied on the owners of stray horses and hogs. Stray horses and hogs were a serious problem. They caused considerable damage to crops and gardens, and the new law was designed to fix two problems. The system of auctioning off care of the poor was subject to horrific abuse, and the revenues raised from dogs, horses, and hogs proved to be insufficient. The colony eventually established almshouses and poorhouses. A poorhouse was a punitive workhouse, and an almshouse was a much less demanding and more charitable shelter.[8]

Poorhouses were a feature of Canadian cities well into the early twentieth century. Fortunately, their quality improved steadily, but during the Confederation era there was considerable variation in the quality of their services. Many poorhouses provided wretched accommodation and treated the "inmates" no differently than criminals. Others were supported by the charity of church parishes, and provided a warm, dry, and comforting place to live. Nonetheless, poorhouses were few in number and space was limited. Consequently, it was not uncommon to commit those with significant intellectual impairments to local jails. It was a cruel practice, as many were shackled in basement cells or housed alongside violent criminals. As the jails became crowded, the mentally challenged were often declared as "dangerous lunatics" and admitted as permanent wards of the state to the provincial lunatic asylum.[9]

While treatment of the poor and mentally challenged has changed over the years, Canadian attitudes on national defence and the military have shown remarkable consistency. Throughout the Confederation era, the only major security threat to Canada came from the United States. Up to that time, Americans had threatened Canada with some regularity. In 1775, Benedict Arnold led an unsuccessful attempt to seize Quebec in one of the opening moves of the American Revolutionary War. Thirty-seven years later, in the War of 1812, as a result

Two enthusiastic militia soldiers from Toronto demonstrate the correct drill for attacking parlour furniture, Toronto, 1870.

of British attempts to restrict U.S. trade and America's desire to expand its territory, U.S. troops mounted several incursions into Canada. A half century after that, Fenians, American Irish veterans of the Civil War, launched several raids into Canada in an attempt to force Britain out of Ireland. Confederation-era Canadians understood that there was a real military threat, and that it had reappeared with a degree of consistency. Nonetheless, Canadians were reluctant to invest in their military forces.

As relations between the United Kingdom and America soured during the Civil War, the British were anxious to see Canada bear some of the cost for its own defence. Sir John A. Macdonald agreed, and introduced a bill to create a trained, equipped, and paid militia of 50,000 men, some of whom could be chosen by a form of conscription. Macdonald's bill was defeated, his government fell, and the ensuing government passed a bill authorizing a militia force of 10,000 inadequately equipped, unpaid volunteers who were to receive a maximum of twelve days training each year. Fortunately, when the Fenians attacked several years later, they did not prove to be a determined enemy. The threat disappeared after a few minor battles, and the American government intervened to prevent further provocations. Despite an enthusiastic response by the militia, the brief conflict showed serious inadequacies in equipment, training, and organization — issues that were well understood beforehand, but assiduously ignored.

As relations with the Americans improved, in 1871, with the exception of small garrisons in Halifax and Esquimalt, the British withdrew all of their troops from North America. To act as a training nucleus for the militia, in the 1870s Canada created a handful of miniscule, undermanned, and underfunded regular army units. The militia provided the troops for the bloodless Red River expedition in 1870. But for the remainder of the period, Canada's army remained untrained, ill equipped, and wracked by patronage.[10] The military's experience during the Confederation era typified Canada's paradoxical and enduring attitudes to defence preparedness: the country relied on more powerful allies for its defence, while maintaining enthusiastic, but the smallest possible peace time forces.

Canada's monetary system and policies have undergone a radical transformation over the years. Long before Confederation, the Canadian monetary system was a jumble of currencies. During the early years of the Confederation decades, if a farmer went to the local general store he would not necessarily have conducted his transactions using British pounds. The pound sterling was not the primary currency. American dollars, British pounds, locally produced bank notes, and bank notes from the Atlantic colonies were all in use, with each of the British North American colonies deciding for itself the value, or "rating," of the various currencies. In 1858, to simplify things, and in a move indicative of the prevailing international trade links, the government of Canada passed a law that all government financial reckonings be tracked in dollars. During that same year, the government issued coins in Canadian denominations.

Prior to Confederation, Canadian dollars were issued and secured by several different regional banks. It was a simple arrangement. There was no central bank; banks had to secure any bills they issued, and the Canadian dollar was generally assumed to be equal to an American dollar. Although several smaller banks failed in the 1850s, causing a brief period of financial uncertainty for Canadian dollars, the system worked reasonably well. After Confederation, the government assumed jurisdiction over currency and banking. In April 1871, with the passage of the Uniform Currency Act, the Canadian government finally replaced all colonial currencies with Canadian dollars.[11] Canada did not create a central bank until 1935, and chartered banks were allowed to continue issuing their own bank notes until 1944.

Chapter Eighteen

EDUCATION, MEDIA, AND THE POPULAR ARTS

As a small frontier nation, Canada did not make a large contribution to the arts during the Confederation era. Canadians were, in comparison to other nations of the period, a very literate population and they valued culture, but it was a small market from which to support any kind of sustained and viable arts community. On the other hand, basic Canadian educational standards were relatively high; and, although no comprehensive literacy tests were conducted in Canada until well into the twentieth century, there is evidence that a substantial percentage of the adult population could read and write. Those who graduated from elementary school generally displayed in their writing a firm grasp of grammar, a broad vocabulary, and a sense of logic and clarity. Contemporary letters and documents indicate a society that was functionally literate, but, in comparison to modern tastes, was somewhat florid in its written expression.[1]

Letter writing was considered to be an art form, and the ability to write an informative and entertaining letter was highly valued. Like so much else during the period, there was a strict etiquette surrounding letter writing. Next to an actual conversation, letter writing was the most important and predominant form of communication. There were numerous references available on the subject of letter writing, detailing everything from correct forms of address to the appropriate timing and frequency of letters to individuals. The quality of a letter was regarded, not unreasonably, as an indicator of the writer's intellect, social standing and sincerity. As a result, painstaking attention was given to their drafting. In our own time, where abbreviating text messages to their simplest possible comprehensible configuration is seen almost as an art form, the letters of the Confederation decades seem to be exaggerated and flamboyant extravagances.

Letter-writing styles were in part a product of the period's educational system. As we've seen, the compulsory period for Canadian education was short, but it was also disciplined and rigorously focused on classical models. For its time, it was one of the best universal education systems in the world. Egerton Ryerson, who was the driving force behind much of English Canada's attitudes to education, was a zealous believer in classical pedagogy. The emphasis in schools, both in English- and French-speaking Canada, was on personal discipline, rote learning, repetitive drills, handwriting skills, arithmetical problem solving, and memorization of lengthy passages from the classics and the Bible. In the higher grades, Latin and Greek were deemed to be an essential part of a rounded education.[2] Although children were divided into grades, most of the schools were rural and had only one teacher instructing everyone. Often in such cases, older students served as "monitors" who oversaw and tutored the younger students. Throughout the period, vocational education was regarded largely as a responsibility of private industry.

Discipline in school was more than just a means to an end. It was considered to be a laudable academic goal in itself, one which was inextricably tied to academic achievement and social progress. Based upon studies in the United States, men like Ryerson believed that literacy was a key factor in reducing the crime rate. It was a belief that led Canadian educators to favour free, high-quality public education that stressed classroom discipline. Nineteenth-century Canadian notions of academic discipline encompassed not only adherence to rules, but discipline was also viewed as a means of

developing the qualities of determination and intellectual tenacity in the general population. Perseverance, steadfastness, and high moral character were thought to be inculcated by rigorous instruction in the three Rs and unremitting exposure to classical teachings. It was also a time when schools were viewed as an opportune means to indoctrinate patriotic and civic values. After 1867, civic education in most Canadian schools stressed loyalty on regional, national, and imperial levels. Love of country and Empire as well as Christian values were stressed in literature, music, history, and geography lessons. There is little evidence of any serious opposition to this instruction, and new immigrants from America as well as mainland Europe showed every indication of being eager to adopt the civic values of their new country.

Although Canadian schools had many similarities to British and American educational programs, curriculums were largely determined by Canadians, and the belief in mass education meant that schooling was for its time generally more accessible to the entire population than it was elsewhere in the English-speaking world.[3]

Newspapers and magazines were popular during the Confederation period, but had nothing remotely close to the relative market penetration of modern media. Canadians of the time lived in a media desert by comparison to their modern counterparts, who are deluged with messages from social media, the internet, television, radio, billboards, magazines, and newspapers.

Canadian newspapers had been in existence for some time before the Confederation decades. French Canada had newspapers from the early eighteenth century, and English Canada had newspapers from the time of the first settlers. As English settlements grew, so too did local newspapers. Halifax, Saint John, Montreal, Kingston, and Toronto all had weekly newspapers, and by the time of Confederation there were scores of Canadian weekly news sheets. Every town that boasted even a bi-weekly flyer usually had two papers: one Liberal and one Conservative. Throughout the period, political opinions were held strongly and virtually every Canadian newspaper had a vigorous, politically partisan perspective.

The 1850s saw the beginnings of two major changes in Canadian newspapers. The introduction of the telegraph meant that, within hours, events from around the world were brought to the reading public's attention. The telegraph was one of the Confederation era's three key technological developments accelerating the transformation of the country's character. Along with the steamship and the train, the telegraph helped moved the country from an insular and regional world view to a more global and dynamic mindset. The first use of the telegraph in Canada was between Toronto and Hamilton in 1842. By 1866, undersea cables linked Newfoundland to Ireland. By the end of the period every sizable community in the country was connected to the rest of the world.

The second significant innovation of the era that had its origins in newspapers was the increased use of commercial advertising. The growth of advertising in Canada occurred only a few short decades after industrialization, and it paralleled almost precisely the growth of newspapers. As the supply of manufactured goods in Canada increased, businesses turned to local newspapers to advertise their wares. It was a move that marked the beginning of Canada's consumer-oriented society. Because of newspapers with their new-found stream of advertising revenue, the country began a pronounced shift to a more commercially oriented culture, one that has remained deeply ingrained in our daily lives. Advertising and an increasingly segmented newspaper industry — which by the 1880s had introduced high-speed web processes, printed photographs, and expanded coverage targeted at numerous segments of the reading public — meant that Canadians began the initial transformation from a frugal rural society characterized by common experiences to a much more individual culture of luxury and consumption.

While Canadian society was showing the very first signs of consumerism, by the end of the Confederation decades, there were notable changes with regard to leisure. Perhaps most importantly, during the later stages of the Confederation era, people, particularly the well-to-do middle classes in cities, found themselves with more time on their hands. As the society became more affluent, personal leisure time grew. And as leisure time increased, so too did interest in group and team sports and sporting clubs. During the latter decades of the period, even individual activities such as skating, hunting, shooting, and snowshoeing were frequently organized in clubs. This probably reflected the period's long-established tendency for people to view themselves in a group context rather than an individual one. Canadians of the Confederation era were confident in their own identities and had few concerns about alienation or the loss of individuality. Despite initial changes in newspapers' market segmentation, daily life was still conducted in small groups, and loss of identification in a mass society was not yet seen to be a psychological threat. It was a time when people readily accepted the company of their peers.

Despite the Confederation generation's undeserved reputation for being restrained and colourless, this member of the Governor General's staff displayed an indisputable sense of panache dressed in his skating costume.

It was also a time when there were no such things as professional sports in Canada. Entertainment was generally seen to be an active endeavour. Spectator sports did not begin to take on anything like their current importance until well into the twentieth century. In fact, Canada's national sport was (and officially still is) lacrosse. Lacrosse was a truly Canadian sport given to us by First Nations, and Canadians, mostly in Montreal, Kingston, Toronto, and Ottawa, took up the game with a passion in the late 1860s and 1870s. Playing lacrosse became a form of patriotic expression and banners posted beside lacrosse fields routinely proclaimed it "Our Country, Our Game." Lacrosse only gradually lost ground to hockey after the Confederation era.

Hockey, which has since become a celebrated national symbol, was in its infancy during the period. Certainly the game as it is played in Canada today had its first formal beginnings in the late nineteenth century. Some credit King's College School in Windsor, Nova Scotia, with the game's invention, while others accept it as an article of faith that the game, as we now know it, originated in contests in Kingston among the Royal Military College, the Royal Canadian Horse Artillery, and Queen's University. Not to be outdone, McGill University has staked a claim that their alumni played the first official games in the 1870s. There may be elements of truth in all of these declarations, for the game evolved and unquestionably began to seize the popular imagination during the final days of the Confederation era. What is without doubt is that it has since become a defining national fixation.

Other sports that Canadians played included cricket, curling, and variations of baseball. Baseball, as played in

Canada at the time, had various rules; some versions of the game had five bases, used cricket bats, and had eleven players per side. The American version of the game became broadly accepted in Ontario in the 1860s.

In addition to sports, Confederation-era Canadians participated in the arts on an amateur basis. The country was not large enough to develop its own elite, commercially successful communities until much later, but the period was nonetheless characterized by individuals actively engaging in events rather than observing them. Music is a good example. Love of music was as equally a universal trait in the Confederation era as it is now. With no recorded music available there was much less variety, but lack of variety did not prevent people from making their own music. Singing, for example, was a more popular and accepted pastime than it is now. Having a good voice was a much-prized social blessing, but it wasn't a prerequisite to having a good time. People sang at home as entertainment, they sang in groups at school and in churches, and they sang without the awkward public discomfort that modern Canadians exhibit when called upon to sing.

Musical instruments were expensive and many years of lessons, although available, were usually only accessible to the affluent urban middle classes. Nevertheless, many families across Canada's broad middle-class spectrum would have scrimped to own one of the new, mass-manufactured pianos. During the Confederation decades, pianos became central features of social life at home. In the days before the gramophone and the radio, public music was a rarity, so Canadian families made and enjoyed their own music. Group singing, or as it was

commonly known, "parlour music," was a stimulating and creative outlet. It was a wonderful way to relieve stress and was an intensely sociable activity. Parlour music was such a highly valued activity that having the ability to play the piano was considered an important social skill for well-to-do young women.

For a small country, Canada had many successful and high-quality piano and organ manufacturers. It was a vigorous industry, well-supported by Canadian and American markets. And while Canadians did a brisk trade in quality keyboard instruments, free trade with the United States also ensured that Canadians were well-supplied with fiddles, banjos, concertinas, and autoharps. These instruments were commonly played and often passed down from one generation to the next with kitchen and parlour musicians learning to play popular tunes by ear.

Regional music flourished in Canada during the Confederation decades. In French-speaking Quebec and Acadia, the Maritimes, and Newfoundland, distinct local versions of Celtic music remained popular. While in English-speaking Quebec, Ontario, and the West, strong American and British music hall influences determined much of the music that was played.

Home or community entertainment also often entailed amateur theatrical performances, which frequently involved preparing elaborate costumes. Amateur dramatic productions were popular, not the least because they took weeks of intense activity to prepare and rehearse. Drawing on centuries-old English traditions of the village pantomime, Confederation-era Canadians often wrote the scripts and scores for their

The interior of a middle-class house in Nova Scotia. The musical instrument is a harmonium, or parlour organ, built in Guelph, Ontario, in the late 1860s.

own theatricals. Sadly, this is a tradition that, except for the locally produced theatrics found in the junior years of grade schools, has all but died out in Canada.

In addition, in the towns and cities, churches and schools often sponsored art exhibitions, drawing classes, textile arts courses, as well as singing and dancing lessons. Reading was a popular form of entertainment, although books were expensive, there were far fewer libraries per capita than there are now, and those that existed during the Confederation decades were fee-based organizations. Tax-supported libraries did not appear in Canada until the first ones were established in Toronto and Saint John in 1883. In many towns there were "Mechanics' Institutes," which provided lectures and reading material in an organized attempt to develop adult education.

The Confederation decades in Canada had a vibrant cultural and artistic life, but in keeping with the largely rural nature of the society, it tended to be family- and community-oriented. This situation would remain largely unchanged until the social upheavals of the First World War.

Chapter Nineteen

CHARACTERISTICS AND IDENTITY

If Canadian society of the Confederation decades had a major, identifiable failing, it was its belief in Darwinian ecology, survival of the fittest and the resulting treatment of aboriginal peoples. There was much that was right and good about the society, but Canada, then as now, has always had a tendency to overlook the desperate situation of our aboriginal peoples. They were the most vulnerable segment of society, one that was shattered by disease, and then deliberately and steadily marginalized and ostracized. While Canadian aboriginal peoples may not have been treated nearly as savagely as aboriginal societies in other lands colonized by Europeans, their circumstances during the period leave no room for self-congratulation.

Notwithstanding this one obvious contention, assessing the shortcomings and strengths of the past using the standards of the present is a risky undertaking. Casting judgment usually means that one views history through the lens of modern values and sensibilities, which is unfair. Surely the best test for accountability is whether or not an individual or group could have known or acted differently at the time. And in this respect, Canadians knew that their treatment of First Nations consistently left aboriginal peoples disconnected, forgotten, and in reduced circumstances — yet at the same time took no sustained or effective measures to fix the situation. This is not just a modern perspective; there were several written accounts of the unease that many felt regarding the treatment of aboriginal peoples.[1]

Apart from this one inescapable judgment, evaluating a society can be a wildly inexact undertaking. This is often because we tend to assess a period by trying to define its values in hindsight. It has recently become popular for politicians and the media to talk at considerable length about Canadian values. But as an overview of the Confederation decades shows, our values have never been constant — nor unanimously held. Values are important, but they change, sometimes quickly, and they are often hard to nail down as people frequently disagree as to what they mean. We have had very different perspectives on such basic concepts as family, religion, race, community, and country. And, no doubt, our attitudes will continue to evolve, probably driven by the same kinds of things that prompted change throughout the Confederation decades. Changes in science, technology, economics, and our understanding of the natural world will almost certainly leave our descendants as amused and puzzled by some of our current notions as we have been by our forebears. So, instead of trying to view the Confederation decades in terms of their values, their situation comes into sharper focus if one looks at their characteristics.

Significantly, the critical characteristics of the period were all highly inter-related. The predominant feature of the Confederation decades was that Canada was a secure country. In relation to the rest of the world, Canada was relatively peaceful, an advantage conferred on the country by geography and circumstances rather than temperament or achievement. Yet, such good fortune had its own associated downstream benefits. Prolonged peace meant that the society was also a relatively stable one. Canada certainly had its share of internal conflicts, but they were insignificant by comparison with most other nations of the period.

Stability, in turn, was reinforced by a respect for the rule of law. Secure, stable societies are more likely to organize themselves around reliable legal institutions than authoritarian or anarchical systems. And Canadians

of all backgrounds were, for the most part, people who respected the law. This respect for laws in turn helped generate a climate of relative prosperity. Pioneers and farmers could cultivate their land comfortable in the knowledge that they had rights and protection from arbitrary arrest, property seizure, and theft.

Prosperity was also closely related to other characteristics. Confederation-era Canada was an agrarian society with a pioneer spirit. With good luck, courage, persistence, and hard work, Canadians could become independent and self-sufficient, which in turn contributed to the country being largely egalitarian in its outlook. Land was virtually free, and there was no landed aristocracy or hereditary governing class. Even though there were economic, religious, and regional divisions, sturdy, self-employed farmers and shopkeepers saw themselves as socially mobile as well as being the political and social equals of one another.

Again, because it was mainly an egalitarian society, Confederation-era Canada was, in its own idiosyncratic, and often contradictory way, fair-minded. With the notable and shameful exceptions of how First Nations were treated, the informal segregation of blacks, and discriminatory practices against Chinese, Canadians were as fair as any other society of the time. Even with the shortcomings that have been noted, there were other signs of progressive and broad-minded behaviour. The number of altruistic volunteers who chose to fight in America's Union Army, the Underground Railroad, and the desire to provide education for First Nations all indicate a leavening of belief across Canadian society that people should be treated with decency and respect. The beginnings of this attitude probably had its origins in the variety of pluralism that the French and English adopted after 1759. Neither side was subservient to the other, and, despite the cultural gap between the two groups, there was a genuine understanding that co-operation, collaboration, and generosity of spirit would result in mutual prosperity.

The very nature of prosperity and the lifestyles of Confederation-era Canadians was also a characteristic feature of the period. People like Walter Ferguson in P.E.I. at the time of the Charlottetown Conference were quite typical. Proud, self-reliant, optimistic, and successful, they lived a frugal life that was close to the land, but relatively free from want. They were literate, and more often than not well read, but not highly educated. They lived within their means in a less technologically sophisticated era and in a pre-consumerist society. In many ways it was also an insular society. Long before the era of mass communications, people relied on speeches, sermons, conversations, and the occasional newspaper or magazine for their information. It was a time that had nothing remotely like our incessant barrage of social media, gossipy information, advertisements, and unceasing political messaging. It was a much simpler era with a happy, uncomplicated outlook that modern, urban Canadians can only envy.

The downside to this lifestyle was the amount of work required to survive. Work-life balance was given short shrift during the period. There were certainly times of levity and recreation, but they were not nearly as frequent as what Canadians would later come to enjoy. Confederation-era Canadians had, of necessity, an unsparing and exacting work ethic.

While the people of the period worked extraordinarily hard, they displayed inconsistent and contradictory attitudes to risk. Canada's explorers in the Arctic and the West during this period, surprisingly, had a high percentage of foreign-born men. Yet paradoxically, this was also a generation that invested heavily in and began building a transcontinental railway before they were even certain that there was a pass through the Rocky Mountains. Today, the most reckless and uninhibited investment banker would probably be punished severely for so much as suggesting such an action.

Because it was a newer, agrarian society, one without large accumulations of capital and wealth, investment in business and industry was also slower and on a proportionately smaller scale than it was in Britain or the United States. And, for similar reasons, with a tiny population made up of an over-worked rural middle class, there were few professional artists of any sort.

Despite all of the common characteristics listed above, most Canadians of the period were not intensely patriotic. Most were proud of their new country, and they were anxious to see it succeed. But strong national identities are normally built over time on such commonalities as ethnicity, language, culture, and religious beliefs. Canada was building a new country, which had none of these as a shared overriding feature. Of the major ethnic groups in the period, the English, the Protestant Irish, and most of the Scots had strong loyalties to Britain and the Empire. French Canadians had steadfast regional and ethnic allegiances to Quebec and Acadia. The Catholic Irish harboured a range of hostile feelings to the very idea of being an independent British colony. And the aboriginal peoples, who were never consulted in the process of making a new country, were generally indifferent to any new administrative arrangements that at the time made no discernable changes to their situation.

Yet, even though the nation's common lifestyles and customs were not apparent at the time, traditions of tolerance, respect, shared hardships, egalitarianism, and collaboration steadily and imperceptibly began to define aspects of the Canadian identity. Not unnaturally, patriotic Canadian feeling took some time to gain traction. While there was enthusiasm virtually everywhere to making the new country work, a vigorous, pervasive, and confident sense of national identity would not emerge for another four decades.

It wasn't until the First World War, when ordinary citizens went abroad in very large numbers, in a common cause, facing horrific perils, that Canadians realized that they already possessed a distinctive and common identity. And while there is no question that the nature of that identity was first revealed on Europe's battlefields, the core of that identity had been forged in the Confederation decades.

Acknowledgements

I am deeply indebted to the Kingston and Frontenac Public Library and the Ontario Inter-Library Loan Service. The staffs of these underfunded and overworked institutions were magnificently unfailing in responding to my numerous requests for information. I am also especially grateful to my editors: to Dominic Farrell, for his eminent good sense, patience, and sound advice; and to my copy editor, Marg Anne Morrison, whose attention to detail is astonishing.

Notes

INTRODUCTION

1. See Michael Crummey, "The Circus Comes to Charlottetown: The Accidental Birth of a Nation," *The Walrus* (September 25, 2014).
2. Parliamentary Debates on the Subject of the Confederation of the British North American Provinces, 3rd Session, 8th Provincial Parliament of Canada (Ottawa: Parliamentary Printers, 1865), 44.
3. For a description of the evolution of colonial self-government see John Manning Ward, *Colonial Self-Government: The British Experience, 1759–1856* (London: Palgrave Macmillan, 1976).

CHAPTER ONE: BACKGROUND TO A NEW NATION

1. Trevor B. McCrisken, "Exceptionalism: Manifest Destiny" in *Encyclopedia of American Foreign Policy*, vol. 2 (New York: Scribner, 2002), 68.

CHAPTER TWO: THE VICTORIAN OUTLOOK

1. See Goldwin Smith, "Lectures on the Study of History," delivered in Oxford 1859–61 (Toronto: Adam, Stevenson & Co., 1873).

CHAPTER FOUR: THE REGIONS AND FIRST PEOPLES: QUEBEC

1. Cole Harris, *The Reluctant Land* (Vancouver: UBC Press, 2008), 44.
2. John A. Dickinson and Brian Young, *A Short History of Quebec* (Montreal: McGill-Queen's University Press, 2008), 84–92.
3. Paul-André Linteau, René Durocher, and Jean-Claude Robert, *Quebec: A History 1867-1929* (Toronto: James Lorimer & Company, 1983), 85.
4. Yvon Desloge, "Behind the Scene of the Lachine Canal Landscape," *Journal of the Society for*

Industrial Archeology, 2013, 7–13.

5. An Act to Amend and Consolidate the Laws Respecting Indians, assented to 12 April 1876, www.aadnc-aandc.gc.ca/DAM/DAM-INTER-HQ/STAGING/texte-text/1876c18_1100100010253_eng.pdf.

CHAPTER FIVE: THE REGIONS AND FIRST PEOPLES: ONTARIO

1. Census Canada, 1880-1881, vol. 1, www.bac-lac.gc.ca/eng/census/1881/pages/search-help.aspx.
2. John E.C. Brierley, "The Co-Existence of Legal Systems in Quebec: Free and Common Socage in Canada's pays de droit civil" in *Les Cahiers de droit,* vol. 20, no. 1–2, 1979, 277–87, www.erudit.org/revue/cd/1979/v20/n1-2/042317ar.pdf.
3. John McCallum, *Unequal Beginnings: Agricultural and Economic Development in Quebec and Ontario until 1870* (Toronto: University of Toronto Press, 1980), 45–46.
4. Ibid., 45–54.
5. See John Douglas Belshaw, *Canadian History: Pre-Confederation* (B.C. Open Textbook Project), Chapter 9, https://opentextbc.ca/preconfederation.
6. John H. Taylor, *Ottawa: An Illustrated History* (Toronto: James Lorimer & Co., 1986), 25–27.
7. Olive Patricia Dickason, *Canada's First Nations: A History of Founding Peoples from Earliest Times* (Toronto: McClelland and Stewart, 1992), 247.
8. Ibid., 237.
9. John S. Milloy, *A National Crime: The Canadian*

Government and the Residential School System (Winnipeg: University of Manitoba Press, 1999), 3.

CHAPTER SIX: THE REGIONS AND FIRST PEOPLES: THE ATLANTIC PROVINCES

1. For an excellent overview of this period see Eric W. Sager and Gerald Panting, *Maritime Capital: The Shipping Industry in Atlantic Canada, 1820–1914* (Montreal: McGill-Queen's University Press, 1990).
2. Joseph Beete Jukes, *Excursions in and About Newfoundland: During the Years 1839 and 1840,* vol. 1 (Cambridge: Cambridge University Press, 2011).

CHAPTER SEVEN: THE REGIONS AND FIRST PEOPLES: THE WEST AND THE NORTH

1. Robert Baker, "Creating Order in the Wilderness: Transplanting the English Law to Rupert's Land, 1835–51," *Law and History Review* (New York: Cambridge University Press, 1999).
2. For a good overview of life on the Prairies, see Gerald Friesen, *The Canadian Prairies: A History* (Toronto: University of Toronto Press, 1984).
3. Dickason, Olive Patricia, *A Concise History of Canada's First Nations,* 2nd ed. (New York: Oxford University Press, 2010), 192–96.
4. James A. Daschuk, *Clearing the Plains: Disease, Politics of Starvation, and the Loss of Aboriginal Life* (Regina: University of Regina Press, 2013), 42.
5. Carl Waldman, *Atlas of the North American Indian* (New York: Checkmark Books, 2009), 206.

6. Stephen Schneider, *Iced: The Story of Organized Crime in Canada* (Toronto: John Wiley & Sons, 2009), 65–69.

7. For the best summary of the issues facing Plains First Nations in Canada during the Confederation decades see Daschuk, *Clearing the Plains*.

8. For an overview of this issue see Robert Boyd, *The Coming of the Spirit of Pestilence: Introduced Infectious Diseases and Population Decline Among Northwest Coast Indians 1774–1874* (Seattle: University of Washington Press, 1999). For the impact of the bubonic plague, its effects and mortality rates, see John Kelly, *The Great Mortality: An Intimate History of the Black Death* (New York: Harper-Collins, 2005).

9. F.W. Howay, W.N. Sage, and H.F. Angus, *British Columbia and the United States: The North Pacific Slope from Fur Trade to Aviation* (Toronto: Ryerson Press, 1942), 235–36.

10. See David A. Morrison and Germain Georges-Hebert, *Inuit: Glimpses of an Arctic Past* (Ottawa: Canadian Museum of Civilization, 1995).

CHAPTER EIGHT: THE IMMIGRANT PEOPLES: THE IRISH

1. W.J. Patterson, *The Dominion of Canada* (Montreal: D. Bentley and Company, 1883), 67, with particulars as to its extent, climate, agricultural resources, fisheries, mines, manufacturing, and other industries; also, details of home and foreign commerce, including a summary of the census of 1881.

2. Paul Gallagher, "How British Free Trade Starved Millions During Ireland's Potato Famine: A Schiller Institute Paper," last modified May 1995, www.schillerinstitute.org/economy/nbw/pot_famine95.html.

3. For a good examination of the response provided at Grosse Isle see James Magnan, *The Voyage of the Naparima* (Dublin: Carraig Books, 1982).

4. For a general overview of the famine see Cecil Woodham-Smith, *The Great Hunger — Ireland, 1845–1849* (London: Penguin Books, 1991).

5. For example, see W. Scott, "The Orange Order and Social Violence in Mid-Nineteenth Century Saint John," *Acadiensis: Journal of the History of the Atlantic Region*, vol. 13, no. 1, autumn 1983, 68–92.

CHAPTER NINE: THE IMMIGRANT PEOPLES: THE SCOTS

1. See Stanford W. Reid, *The Scottish Tradition in Canada* (Toronto: McClelland and Stewart, 1976).

2. For an overview of the nature of the Scottish Enlightenment see Tom Devine, *Scotland's Empire, 1600–1815* (London: Allen Lane, 2003).

3. H. Pelling, *Social Geography of British Elections, 1885–1910* (London: Palgrave Macmillan, 1967), 373.

4. Ken McGoogan, *Celtic Lightning: How the Scots and the Irish Created a Canadian Nation* (Toronto: Harper-Collins, 2015).

CHAPTER TEN: THE IMMIGRANT PEOPLES: THE FRENCH

1. Claude Bélanger, "The Roman Catholic Church and Quebec," Department of History, Marianopolis College, http://faculty.marianopolis.edu/c.belanger/quebechistory/readings/church.htm.
2. "The History of Acadia," in *The Canadian Encyclopaedia*, www.thecanadianencyclopedia.ca/en/article/history-of-acadia.

CHAPTER TWELVE: THE IMMIGRANT PEOPLES: THE ERA'S NEW MINORITIES

1. John Baker, "The Last of Those Who Had Been Born in Slavery in Canada," in J.F. Pringle, Judge County Court, *Lunenburgh, or the Old Eastern District*, 1890, ch. 36, 1890, http://my.tbaytel.net/bmartin/jbaker.htm.

CHAPTER FOURTEEN: URBAN LIFE

1. Joel Tarr and Clay McShane, "The Horse & the Urban Environment," in *The Environmental Literacy Council*, http://enviroliteracy.org/environment-society/transportation/the-horse-the-urban-environment.
2. Shannon Kyles, Ontario Architecture Website, www.ontarioarchitecture.com/gothicrevival.html.

CHAPTER FIFTEEN: DOMESTIC LIFE

1. Jonathan Hart, *Empires and Colonies* (Cambridge: Polity Press, 2008), 251.
2. Richard Gwyn, "Sir John A. Macdonald, the Greatest PM of All," *Toronto Star*, Insight, January 9, 2015, www.thestar.com/news/insight/2015/01/09/sir_john_a_macdonald_the_greatest_pm_of_all.html.
3. Heather Come Murray, *Bright Improvement! The Literary Societies of Nineteenth-Century Ontario* (Toronto: University of Toronto Press, 2002), 108.
4. Eric W. Sager, "The Transformation of the Canadian Domestic Servant, 1871–1931, Social Science History," in *Cambridge Journals Online*, http://journals.cambridge.org/action/displayAbstract?fromPage=online&aid=10038872.
5. Françoise Noël, *Family Life and Sociability in Upper and Lower Canada, 1780–1870: A View from Diaries and Family Correspondence* (Montreal: McGill-Queen's University Press, 2003), 273–77.
6. See Catharine Parr Strickland Traill, *The Canadian Settler's Guide* (Charleston, NC: Biblio Life, 2014), 28.
7. Lorna F. Hurl, "Restricting Child Factory Labour in Late Nineteenth Century Ontario," in *Labour / Le Travail*, vol. 21, 1988, Athabaska University Press, https://journals.lib.unb.ca/index.php/LLT/article/view/4675.
8. Ibid., 103.
9. Paul Axelrod, *The Promise of Schooling: Education in Canada, 1800–1914* (Toronto: University of Toronto Press, ebook, 1997).

10. For a good overview of this topic, see Una Abrahamson, *God Bless Our Home: Domestic Life in Nineteenth Century Canada* (Toronto: Burns & MacEachern, 1966).

11. Several good essays describing the nature of alcohol use in nineteenth-century Canada can be found in Cheryl Krasnick Warsh, *Drink in Canada: Historical Essays* (Montreal: McGill-Queen's University Press, 1993).

12. Wendy Moss, Elaine Gardner-O'Toole, *Aboriginal People: History of Discriminatory Laws*, Law and Government Division, Library of Parliament, Parliament of Canada, 1991, www.bdp.parl.gc.ca/Content/LOP/ResearchPublicationsArchive/bp1000/bp175-e.asp.

13. Jack S. Blocker, David M. Fahey, and Ian R. Tyrrell, *Alcohol and Temperance in Modern History: An International Encyclopedia* (Santa Barbara: ABC-CLIO, 2003).

14. Cynthia Simpson, "The Treatment of Halifax's Poorhouse Dead During the Nineteenth and Twentieth Centuries," MA Thesis (Halifax: St. Mary's University, 2011), 69.

CHAPTER SIXTEEN: ATTITUDES AND BELIEFS

1. 1871 Census, Statistics Canada, Population tables, 1871–1941, www66.statcan.gc.ca/eng/1943-44/194301780108_p.%20108.pdf.

2. John Henry Newman, *The Idea of a University* (London: Aeterna Press, 2005), 10.

3. Charles Kingsley, *The Works of Charles Kingsley*, vol. 19 (London: Macmillan, 1880), 308.

4. Wilson J. Brent, "Military Aid to the Civil Authority in Mid-19th Century New Brunswick," in *Canadian Military History*, vol. 17, no. 2, April 2012, http://scholars.wlu.ca/cgi/viewcontent.cgi?article=1484&context=cmh.

5. William Smyth, *Toronto, the Belfast of Canada: The Orange Order and the Shaping of Municipal Culture* (Toronto: University of Toronto Press, 2015), 136.

6. Elinor Kyte Senior, "The Gavazzi Riot of 1853," in *British Regulars in Montreal: An Imperial Garrison, 1834–1854* (Montreal: McGill-Queen's University Press, 1981), 109–33.

7. Owen Carrigan, "The Evolution of Juvenile Justice in Canada," for the Canadian Department of Justice, 2, www.justice.gc.ca/eng/rp-pr/csj-sjc/ilp-pji/jj2-jm2/jj2-jm2.pdf.

8. Ibid., 11.

9. Ibid., 7.

10. Marc Alain and Julie Desrosiers, "A Fairly Short History of Youth Criminal Justice in Canada," in *Implementing and Working with the Youth Criminal Justice Act across Canada*, Marc Alain, Raymond R. Corrado, Susan Reid, eds. (Toronto: University of Toronto Press, 2016).

11. Christopher Moore, "That's History: Inventing the Court of Appeal," *in Law Times Digital Editions*, www.lawtimesnews.com/200806092422/commentary/thats-history-inventing-the-court-of-appeal.

CHAPTER SEVENTEEN: INSTITUTIONAL LIFE

1. The British North America Act, Section 92, paragraph 16.
2. John Haligan, *Civil Service Systems in Anglo American Countries* (Cheltenham, UK: Edward Elgar Publishing, 2003), 31–32.
3. For an overview of the last decade of the era, see also Geoffrey Reaume, *Remembrance of Patients Past: Life at the Toronto Hospital for the Insane, 1870–1940* (Toronto: University of Toronto Press, 2000).
4. Kathleen Kendall, "Criminal Lunatic Women in 19th Century Canada," School of Medicine, University of Southampton, www.csc-scc.gc.ca/research/forum/e113/113l_e.pdf.
5. Janet Miron, *Prisons, Asylums, and the Public: Institutional Visiting in the Nineteenth Century* (Toronto: University of Toronto Press, 2011), 32.
6. Michael Welch, *Corrections: A Critical Approach* (London: Routledge, 2013), 42.
7. Peter Oliver, *Terror to Evil-Doers: Prisons and Punishment in Nineteenth-Century Ontario* (Toronto: Osgoode Society for Canadian Legal History, 1998), 350.
8. See Greenhous Brereton, "Paupers and Poorhouses: The Development of Poor Relief in Early New Brunswick," in *Histoire Sociale / Social History*, no. 1, Avril/April 1968 (Ottawa: Université d'Ottawa / Carleton University), 162.
9. See James E. Moran, *Committed to the State Asylum: Insanity and Society in Nineteenth-Century Quebec and Ontario* (Montreal: McGill-Queen's University Press, 2001).
10. J.L. Granatstein, *Canada's Army: Waging War and Keeping the Peace* (Toronto: University of Toronto Press, 2002), 18–27.
11. For a concise overview history of Canada's banking systems, see James Powell, *A History of the Canadian Dollar* (Ottawa: Bank of Canada, 2005), www.bankofcanada.ca/wp-content/uploads/2010/07/dollar_book.pdf.

CHAPTER EIGHTEEN: EDUCATION, MEDIA, AND THE POPULAR ARTS

1. To get a good sense of the writing styles of the period, the most accessible source of Confederation-era documents, with several million documents digitized, is at Early Canadiana Online, http://eco.canadiana.ca.
2. Suzanne de Castell, Allan Luke, Kieran Egan, *Literacy, Society, and Schooling: A Reader* (New York: Cambridge University Press, 1986).
3. See Alison Prentice, *The School Promoters: Education and Social Class in Mid-Nineteenth Century Upper Canada* (Toronto: University of Toronto Press, 2004).

CHAPTER NINETEEN: CHARACTERISTICS AND IDENTITY

1. The impact of white society on aboriginal peoples was well-known and clearly understood from the earliest days of the era. For example, Susanna

Moodie wrote in the early 1850s: "It is a melancholy truth and deeply to be lamented that the vicinity of European settlers has always produced a very demoralizing effect on the Indians." For the full context of this see Susanna Moodie, *Roughing it in the Bush: Or, Life in Canada* (Toronto: Prospero Books, 2000), 36.

Bibliography

Baldwin, Douglas and Spira Thomas. *Gaslights and Vagabond Cows: Charlottetown in the Victorian Era.* Charlottetown: Ragweed Press, 1988.

Bartlett, Richard H. *Indian Reserves and Aboriginal Lands in Canada: A Homeland.* Saskatoon: University of Saskatchewan Native Law Centre, 1990.

Beattie, Susan. *A New Life in Canada: The Letters of Sophia Eastwood, 1843–1870.* Toronto: Canadian Scholars Press, 1989.

Bothwell, Robert. *Canada and Quebec.* Vancouver: UBC Press, 1995.

Boyko, John. *Blood and Daring: How Canada Fought the American Civil War and Forged a Nation.* Toronto: Knopf Canada, 2013.

Boyle, Terry. *Hidden Ontario: Secrets from Ontario's Past.* Toronto: Dundurn Press, 2011.

Bradford, Robert. *Keeping Ontario Moving: The History of Roads and Road Building in Ontario.* Toronto: Dundurn Press, 2015.

Braq, Charlemange Jean. *The Evolution of French Canada.* New York: Macmillan Company, 1924.

Cadigan, Sean T. *Newfoundland & Labrador: A History.* Toronto: University of Toronto Press, 2009.

Campey, Lucille H. *The Scottish Pioneers of Upper Canada 1784–1855.* Toronto: Natural Heritage Books, 2005.

Careless, J.M.S. *The Pioneers: An Illustrated History of Early Settlement in Canada.* Toronto: McClelland and Stewart, 1973.

Carrigan, D. Owen. *Crime and Punishment in Canada: A History.* Toronto: McClelland and Stewart, 1991.

Carter, Sarah. *Aboriginal People and Colonizers of Western Canada to 1900.* Toronto: University of Toronto Press, 1999.

Courville, Serge and Normand Séguin. *Rural Life in Nineteenth-Century Quebec*. Ottawa: Canadian Historical Association, 1989.

Creighton, Donald. *Dominion of the North: A History of Canada*. Toronto: Houghton Mifflin Company, 1944.

————. *The Empire of the St. Lawrence: A Study in Commerce and Politics*. Toronto: University of Toronto Press, 2002.

Daschuk, James A. *Clearing the Plains: Disease Politics of Starvation and the Loss of Aboriginal Life*. Regina: University of Regina Press, 2013.

Dickason, Olive Patricia. *Canada's First Nations: A History of Founding Peoples from Earliest Times*. Toronto: McClelland and Stewart, 1992.

Downie, Mary Alice, Barbara Robertson, and Elizabeth J. Errington. *Early Voices: Portraits of Canada by Women Writers, 1639–1914*. Toronto: Dundurn Press, 2010.

Downs, Ary. *The Law and the Lawless: Frontier Justice on the Canadian Prairies*. Victoria: Heritage House Publishing, 2014.

Elliott, Bruce S. *Irish Migrants in the Canadas: A New Approach*. Montreal: McGill-Queen's University Press, 2004.

Fingard, Judith. *The Dark Side of Life in Victorian Halifax*. Halifax: Pottersfield Press, 1989.

Flanders, Judith. *Inside the Victorian Home*. New York: W.W. Norton and Company, 2003.

Fleming, Patricia. *History of the Book in Canada*. Toronto: University of Toronto Press, 2004.

Fowler, Marian. *The Embroidered Tent: Five Gentlewomen in Early Canada*. Toronto: House of Anansi, 1982.

Friesen, Gerald. *The Canadian Prairies: A History*. Toronto: University of Toronto Press, 1984.

Gagan, David. *Hopeful Travellers: Families, Land, and Social Change in Mid-Victorian Peel County, Canada West*. Toronto: University of Toronto Press, 1981.

Garrick, Alan Bailey and William C. Sturtevant. *Handbook of North American Indians: Indians in Contemporary Society*. Washington: Smithsonian Institution, Government Printing Office, 2008.

Gentilcore, R. Louis. *Historical Atlas of Canada: The Land Transformed, 1800–1891*. Toronto: University of Toronto Press, 1993.

Gerson, Carole and Kathy Mezei, eds. *The Prose of Life: Sketches from Victorian Canada*. Toronto: ECW Press, 1981.

Gold, Wilmer. *Logging as It Was*. Victoria: Morris Publishing, 1985.

Gossage, Peter and J.L. Little. *An Illustrated History of Quebec: Tradition and Modernity*. Toronto: Oxford University Press, 2012.

Gray, Charlotte. *Sisters in the Wilderness: The Lives of Susanna Moodie and Catharine Parr Traill*. Toronto: Penguin Books, 1999.

Greer, Allan. *The People of New France*. Toronto: University of Toronto Press, 1997.

Groulx, Chanoine Lionel. *Histoire du Canada*, 2. Ottawa: Fides, 1960.

Guillet, Edwin C. *Pioneer Days in Upper Canada*. Toronto: University of Toronto Press, 1933.

Gwyn, Richard. *John A. Macdonald: The Man Who Made Us*. Toronto: Random House Canada, 2007.

Haight, Canniff. *Country Life in Canada*. Belleville, ON: Mike Publishing, 1986.

Harman, Donald in Graeme Morton and David A. Wilson, eds. *The Great European Migration and Indigenous Populations in Irish and Scottish Encounters with Indigenous Peoples*. Montreal: McGill-Queen's University Press, 2013.

Hayes, Derek. *Canada: An Illustrated History*. Vancouver: Douglas & McIntyre, 2004.

_____. *Historical Atlas of North American Railroad*. Berkeley: University of California Press, 2010.

Hind, Henry Youle. *Narrative of the Canadian Red River Exploring Expedition of 1857 and of the Assiniboine and Saskatchewan Exploring Expedition of 1858*. London: Longman, Green, Longman, and Roberts, 1860.

Hoffman, Frances and Ryan Taylor. *Much to Be Done: Private Life in Ontario from Victorian Diaries*. Toronto: Natural Heritage Books, 1996.

Jones, Mary Fallis. *The Confederation Generation*. Toronto: Royal Ontario Museum, 1978.

Lawrence, Bonita. *Fractured Homeland: Federal Recognition and Algonquin Identity in Ontario*. Vancouver: UBC Press, 2012.

Linteau, Paul-Andre. *The History of Montreal: The History of a Great North American City*. Montreal: Baraka Books, 2007.

MacDougall, Robert. *The Emigrants Guide to North America*. Toronto: Natural Heritage Books, 1998.

McCallum, John. *Unequal Beginnings: Agricultural and Economic Development in Quebec and Ontario Until 1870*. Toronto: University of Toronto Press, 1980.

McCord, Norman. *The Anti-Corn Law League, 1838–1846*. London: George Allen & Unwin, 1958.

McCrady, David G. *Living with Strangers: The Nineteenth Century Sioux and the Canadian American Borderlands*. Toronto: University of Toronto Press, 2010.

McGoogan, Ken. *Celtic Lightning: How the Scots and Irish Created a Canadian Nation*. Toronto: Harper-Collins, 2015.

_____. *How the Scots Invented Canada*. Toronto: Harper-Collins, 2010.

McKillop, A.B. *A Disciplined Intelligence: Critical Inquiry and Canadian Thought in the Victorian Era*. Montreal: McGill-Queen's University Press, 1979.

McMillan, Alan D. and Eldon Yellowhorn. *First Peoples in Canada*. Vancouver: Douglas & McIntyre, 2004.

McMullen, John Mercier. *The History of Canada: From Its First Discovery to the Present Time*. Brockville, ON: McMullen & Company, 1868.

Miller, J.R. *Skyscrapers Hide the Heavens: A History of Indian-White Relations in Canada*. Toronto: University of Toronto Press, 2000.

Moodie, Susanna. *Roughing It in the Bush*. Toronto: Prospero Books, 2000.

Morton, Desmond. *A Short History of Canada*. Edmonton: Hurtig Publishers, 1983.

Morton, Graeme and David A. Wilson. *Irish and Scottish Encounters with Indigenous Peoples*. Montreal: McGill-Queen's University Press, 2013.

Neary, Peter and Patrick O'Flaherty. *Part of the Main: An Illustrated History of Newfoundland and Labrador*. St. John's: Breakwater Books, 1983.

Nickerson, Janice. *Crime and Punishment in Upper Canada*. Toronto: Dundurn Press, 2010.

Noel, Francoise. *Family Life and Sociability in Upper and Lower Canada, 1780-1870*. Montreal: McGill-Queen's University Press, 2003.

Osborne, S.L. *In the Shadow of the Pole: An Early History of Arctic Expeditions, 1871-1912*. Toronto: Dundurn Press, 2013.

Palliser, John. *Solitary Rambles and Adventures of a Hunter in the Prairies*. London: John Murray, 1853.

Poulter, Gillian. *Becoming Native in a Foreign Land: Sport, Visual Culture, and Identity in Montreal, 1840-85*. Vancouver: UBC Press, 2010.

Preston, David L. *The Texture of Contact: European and Indian Settler Communities on the Frontiers of Iroquoia, 1667-1783*. Lincoln: University of Nebraska Press, 2009.

Punch, Terrence M. *Erin's Sons: Irish Arrivals in Atlantic Canada 1761-1853*. Baltimore: Genealogical Publishing, 2009.

Reader, W.J. *Life in Victorian England*. New York: Putnam, 1963.

Reid, Stanford W. *The Scottish Tradition in Canada*. Toronto: McClelland and Stewart, 1976.

Rhys, Captain Horton. *A Theatrical Trip for a Wager!* Vancouver: The Alcuin Society, 1966.

Roy, Patricia E. and John Herd Thompson. *British Columbia: Land of Promises*. Toronto: Oxford University Press, 2005.

Sager, Eric W. and Gerald Panting. *Maritime Capital: The Shipping Industry in Atlantic Canada, 1820-1914*. Montreal: McGill-Queen's University Press, 1990.

Saul, John Ralston. *A Fair Country: Telling Truths About Canada*. Toronto: Penguin Books, 2009.

Schlereth, Thomas J. *Victorian America: Transformations in Everyday Life, 1876-1915*. Toronto: Harper Perennial, 1992.

Sendzikas, Aldona. *Stanley Barracks: Toronto's Military Legacy*. Toronto: Dundurn Press, 2011.

Simpson, Cynthia. "The Treatment of Halifax's Poor House Dead During the Nineteenth and Twentieth Centuries." (Thesis, Atlantic Canada Studies.) Halifax: Saint Mary's University, 2011.

Skelton, Isabel. *The Backwoodswoman: A Chronicle of Pioneer Home Life in Upper and Lower Canada*. Toronto: Ryerson Press, 1929.

Taylor, G.W. *Builders of British Columbia: An Industrial History.* Victoria: Morris Publishing, 1982.

Thomson, Colin A. *Blacks in Deep Snow: Black Pioneers in Canada.* Toronto: J.M. Dent and Sons, 1979.

Thorner, Thomas, ed. *A Few Acres of Snow: Documents in Pre-Confederation Canadian History.* Peterborough, ON: Broadview Press, 2003.

Trofimenkoff, Susan Mann. *The Dream of a Nation: A Social and Intellectual History of Quebec.* Toronto: Macmillan Canada, 1982.

Trudel, Marcel. *Canada's Forgotten Slaves: Two Hundred Years of Bondage.* Montreal: Vehicule Press, 2009.

Tulchinsky, Gerald. *Canada's Jews.* Toronto: University of Toronto Press, 2008.

_____. *Taking Root: The Origins of the Canadian Jewish Community.* Toronto: Malcolm Lester Publishing, 1992.

Vance, Jonathan F. *A History of Canadian Culture.* Toronto: Oxford University Press, 2009.

Vroom, Richard. *Old New Brunswick: A Victorian Portrait.* Toronto: Oxford University Press, 1978.

Waite, P.B. *The Life and Times of Confederation: 1864-1867.* Toronto: University of Toronto Press, 1962.

_____. *Macdonald: His Life and World.* Toronto: McGraw Hill Ryerson, 1975.

Ward, Donald. *The People: An Historical Guide to the First Nations of Alberta, Saskatchewan, and Manitoba.* Edmonton: Fifth House, 1995.

Ward, Peter. *Courtship, Love, and Marriage in Nineteenth-Century English Canada.* Montreal: McGill-Queen's University Press, 1993.

Woodham-Smith, Cecil. *The Great Hunger — Ireland, 1845-1849.* London: Penguin Books, 1991.

Wright J.V. *A History of Native People of Canada.* Ottawa: Canadian Museum of Civilization, 1995.

Wright, Richard Thomas. *In a Strange Land: A Pictorial Record of the Chinese in Canada, 1788-1923.* Saskatoon: Western Producer Prairie Books, 1988.

Year-Book and Almanac of British North America for 1867. Montreal: Lowe and Chamberlin Printing House, 1867.

Zeller, Suzanne. *Inventing Canada: Early Victorian Science and the Idea of a Transcontinental Nation.* Toronto: University of Toronto Press, 1987.

Image Credits

All images courtesy of Library and Archives Canada

Index

Numbers in italics indicate images.